end to torment

Photograph of H. D. by Ezra Pound

end to torment H.D.
A memoir of Ezra Pound by

Edited by *Norman Holmes Pearson and Michael King*

With the poems from "Hilda's Book" by
EZRA POUND

A NEW DIRECTIONS BOOK

This volume was published with the co-operation of the Center for the
Study of Ezra Pound and His Contemporaries, in the Beinecke Library of
Yale University. "Hilda's Book" appears by permission of the Houghton
Library, Harvard University.

Manufactured in the United States of America
New Directions books are printed on acid-free paper
First published clothbound and as New Directions Paperbook 476 in 1979
Published simultaneously in Canada by Penguin Books Canada Limited

Library of Congress Cataloging in Publication Data

Doolittle, Hilda, 1886–1961.
    End to torment.
    (A New Directions Book)
    Includes bibliographical references.
    1. Pound, Ezra Loomis, 1885–1972—Biography. 2. Doolittle, Hilda,
1886–1961—Friends and associates. 3. Poets, American—20th century—Bi-
ography. I. H. D. II. D., H. III. Pound, Ezra Loomis, 1885–1972.
Hilda's book. 1979. IV. Pearson, Norman Holmes, 1909–1975. V. King,
Michael John. VI. Title.
ps3531.082z595 1979   811'.5'2 [B]   78-27149
isbn 0–8112–0719–6
isbn 0–8112–0720–X pbk.

New Directions Books are published for James Laughlin
by New Directions Publishing Corporation,
80 Eighth Avenue, New York 10011

THIRD PRINTING

CONTENTS

Foreword by Michael King   vii

End to Torment   3

"Hilda's Book" by Ezra Pound   67

FOREWORD

This book has been twenty years in the making, and in its brief compass recounts a friendship, a romance, and a collaboration in poetry reaching back to the beginning of the century. Ezra Pound and Hilda Doolittle began the century together, in Pennsylvania, and though their European odysseys carried them in separate directions, throughout the years they maintained their friendship. Their final correspondence recalls their earliest days together; H.D.'s last letters to Pound are signed "Dryad," the name he had given her when they were young. H.D.'s daughter, Perdita Schaffner, has written of that time:

> They were young together, young poets together, innovators, close friends. It was he who suggested she use her initials as a byline. She felt that her own name invited puns and facetious jokes. H.D. it was, she was, from then on. They considered marriage. Their betrothal was tentative and unofficial, strongly opposed by her family, and eventually broken off . . .[1]

The story of the professional collaboration of the two young poets has been told many times: how Pound contrived the school of "imagiste" poetry at least partly to describe the specific qualities of H.D.'s early poems and to help get those poems into print. Later, as she records in this memoir, the continuing influence of Pound's *Cantos* helped her find a form for her own long poems, *Trilogy* and *Helen in Egypt*. And one of her last poems, "Winter Love," written shortly after *End to Torment,* transfigures their early love into a mythical relation between Helen and Odysseus. Characteristically, H.D. apprehended a symbolic or universal pattern underlying her own experience and attempted in her writing to give that pattern expression.

End to Torment, although an intensely personal memoir, shows some of the same techniques and habits of mind. She had written of the artist Undine to Norman Holmes Pearson, as she was composing the memoir: "I want to work this out as it touches (very distantly) my own shock at Ezra leaving for Europe—1908?"[2] And she connects Pound's political isolation and imprisonment, after World War II, with the reaction of the staid Philadelphia community to his return from Indiana, where he had resigned his position as an instructor at Wabash College after a minor scandal. Hilda was loyal to Ezra then, although when she asked him about the malicious rumors, he responded with his characteristic gifts of defiance and self-dramatization: "They say that I am bi-sexual and given to unnatural lust."

At the time of writing *End to Torment* (1958), H.D. found herself, once again, nearly alone among her companions in her defense of her fellow poet. Her friends Bryher and Sylvia Beach understandably resented Pound's wartime activities and sympathies and discouraged her from engaging in apologetics. She herself had no wish to add to the unhealthy publicity surrounding Pound, "on top of the journalists."[3] But while there was no haste for publication, her longtime friend and literary adviser Norman Holmes Pearson encouraged her to record her recollections at this crucial time, when the continuing efforts to arrange Pound's release from Federal custody seemed finally near success. The good news came even while the manuscript was in progress, in a letter from Pearson: "And now another canyon has been bridged by Ezra's end to torment."

Another ally in the struggle to remember was H.D.'s doctor, Erich Heydt, whom she met at the Klinik Hirslanden in Küsnacht, Switzerland. His role in the recollections is well documented in the memoir itself. Most importantly, H.D. herself felt the need to recall and express memories that would otherwise be lost forever. She wrote to Pearson:

> [Your letter] has given me back the early American scene, when almost everyone I knew in Philadelphia was against him, after that Wabash college *débacle*. Erich always said I was "hiding something." It was all *that,* my deep love for Ezra, complicated by family (& friends) lack of sympathy—my inner schism—outwardly, I went on, after E. (1908) went to Venice. I have been writing of this & Erich has been helping me . . . I *did* have a life in U.S. . . .
>
> I have E.P. books piled on my table. I had to try to hide them—& talk of everything but what most deeply concerned me. . . . I have been so *happy* writing the *E.P.* "story"—it must not be taken away from me . . . poor, poor Ezra. Only now, with the hope of his release, dare I go back & on. "It is so long ago," I say to Erich. "No," he says, "it is existentialist," (his word) "eternal."[4]

The "existential" quality of *End to Torment* is emphasized by its journal form, which mingles memories with the circumstances of recollection, allowing H.D. to catch resonances which connect past and present. She remembers how the young Ezra reminded her of Paderewski, whom she had heard in concert as a girl; and a red-haired child glimpsed in a railway station, or a young pianist (Van Cliburn) on a tour of Europe, becomes the "spirit-child" that she and Ezra might have had. The form is similar to that used in her *Tribute to Freud* (New York, 1956; revised edition, Boston, 1974), a journal-essay on her psychoanalysis and her own mythic approach to psychic mysteries. *End to Torment* can be read as a personal sequel to *Tribute to Freud,* and ironically its methods contrast sharply with the resolutely impersonal, intellectual attitudes of Pound. H.D. refers deferentially and comically to a letter from Pound in which he decries her interest in the "pig-sty" of Freudian psychology.

Throughout the memoir runs H.D.'s conviction that her life and Ezra's had been intertwined irrevocably since those early days when they walked together, "maenad and bassarid," in the Pennsylvania woods, and he wrote for her poems imitating William Morris, Rossetti, and Swinburne, even Chaucer. (Twenty-five of those poems, handbound in vellum by Pound and titled "Hilda's Book," are first published here as an epilogue to her memoir of their first love.) Pound goaded her own ambition to write poetry, and his mock-Bohemian manner, his bad luck in his attempt to become a respectable professor, and his romantic departure for Europe under a cloud of disgrace seemed to fulfill the plangent historical novels they had read together. In a few years she followed him, for a summer visit that became a lifetime. "I was separated from my friends, my family, even from America, by Ezra." Paradoxically, the recounting of Pound's own confinement in St. Elizabeth's and the imminence of his eventual release turn her thoughts homeward and tie her to America still: "I feel so violently American, in the pro-Ezra sense, though it has gone so badly with him."

As she was writing the journal that became *End to Torment,* her friends kept her supplied with news from America and reports on visits to the "Ezuversity," as Pound called his circle at St. Elizabeth's Hospital. Erich had stopped there on a cross-country tour; Richard Aldington, her former husband, sent an article from *The Nation* ("Weekend with Ezra Pound") which treated Pound with some sympathetic understanding. She ran across another piece in the German periodical *Merkur* and read the correspondence in *Poetry* that defended Pound against political slander. The signs seemed to indicate that the atmosphere had changed enough, since the war, so that Pound could soon be set free. Her final entry quotes a letter from Pearson, recounting his farewell visit with the Pounds in a cabin on the *Cristoforo Colombo,* soon bound for Italy.

H.D.'s version of the past and present is characteristically enigmatic and emotionally transcendent. "It is the *feel* of things rather than what people do. It runs through all the poets, really, of the world. One of *us* had been trapped. Now, one of *us* is free." The journal ends with Pound's freedom, and a rose given by Pearson in H.D.'s name "for the Paradiso." In the subsequent months, H.D. sent the manuscript to Brunnenburg, Italy, for Pound's comments, and he responded with a few suggestions and the note, "there is a great deal of beauty."[5] A few days later he added a touching postscript: "Torment title excellent, but optimistic."[6]

Norman Holmes Pearson encouraged H.D. to complete the memoir, gave it a title, and was preparing it for publication when he died in 1975. (The manuscript is now a part of the Yale Collection of American Literature in the Beinecke Rare Book and Manuscript Library.) H.D. had written to E.P., "I dedicated it to 'Norman,' *he wanted me to write it.*"[7] There had been a false start some years before, when in 1950 she had written a short recollection for a book Peter Russell was editing for Pound's sixty-fifth birthday. That was never published, and it is due to Pearson's attentiveness and energy that we have this longer record of the friendship of two of the most important poets of the century. The publication also includes "Hilda's Book" (which H.D. here calls "the Hilda Book"), the "little book" handbound by Pound and given to Hilda. She had thought it lost during the war in London, where it had been in the keeping of her friend Frances Gregg, but it was saved and eventually came into the hands of Peter Russell, who sold it to the Houghton Library of Harvard University. We are grateful for their permission to reprint it here.

This publication is a project sponsored by the Center for the Study of Ezra Pound and His Contemporaries, in the Beinecke Library of Yale University. I am grateful to Donald Gallup and Louis Martz for their advice and assistance in the preparation of this text.

M.K.

Notes

[1] Perdita Schaffner, "Merano, 1962," in *Paideuma,* vol. 4, no. 2/3, Fall-Winter 1975, p. 513.

[2] Letter from H.D. to Norman Holmes Pearson, June 3, 1958. In the Collection of American Literature [C.A.L.], Beinecke Library, Yale University.

[3] Letter from H.D. to Ezra Pound, January 2, 1959. C.A.L., Beinecke Library, Yale University.

[4] Letter from H.D. to Norman Holmes Pearson, April 11, 1958. C.A.L., Beinecke Library, Yale University.

[5] Letter from Ezra Pound to H.D., November 6, 1959. C.A.L., Beinecke Library, Yale University.

[6] Letter from Ezra Pound to H.D., November 13, 1959. C.A.L., Beinecke Library, Yale University.

[7] Letter from H.D. to Ezra Pound, January 2, 1959. C.A.L., Beinecke Library, Yale University.

end to torment

for Norman

[*Küsnacht*]¹
Friday
March 7, 1958

Snow on his beard. But he had no beard, then. Snow blows down from pine branches, dry powder on the red gold. "I make five friends for my hair, for one for myself."

Or did he wear a soft hat, a cap pulled down over his eyes? A mask, a disguise? His eyes are his least impressive feature. But am I wrong? They seem small; color? Pebble-green? Surely not an insignificant feature. Gothic, as they call it, moonlight drifts through these etched trees. Cold?

Some sort of *rigor mortis*. I am frozen in this moment.

Perhaps I held it all my life, it is what they called my "imagery"; even now, they speak of "verse so chiselled as to seem lapidary," and they say, "She crystallizes—that is the right word." They say, "that is the right word." This moment must wait 50 years for the right word. Perhaps he had said it; perhaps in the frost of our mingled breath, the word was written. He was maybe nineteen, I was a year younger [*1905—Ed.*]. Immensely sophisticated, immensely superior, immensely rough-and-ready, a product not like any of the brothers and brothers' friends—and boys we danced with (and he danced badly). One would dance with him for what he might say. It didn't matter, with a lot of people around. Here, in the winter woods, it seemed significant.

It seemed at the same time, infinitely trivial—was he showing off? Why must he say it? He said, "She said, 'Have you ever kissed a girl before?' I said, 'Never under the Rock of Gibraltar.'"

No need, then, to ask the question. First kisses? In the

woods, in the winter—what did one expect? Not this. Electric, magnetic, they do not so much warm, they magnetize, vitalize. We need never go back. Lie down under the trees. Die here. We are past feeling cold; isn't that the first symptom of *rigor mortis?*

They used to say, "Run around, children; it's all right as long as you don't stop running." Had I stopped running?

Stop running for a moment, if you dare call him back.

There are very few left who know what he looked like then. There is a hint of a young, more robust Ignace Paderewski[2] or even of the tawny Swinburne, if his frail body had ever reached maturity. But this young (already) iconoclast is rougher, tougher than the Polish poet or the Border bard. It is whispered among us that he "writes," but he has not spoken of this to me yet. "Where are you? Come back—," is shouted by the crowd above on the icy toboggan-run. "Shout back," I say and he gives a parody of a raucous yodel, then "Haie! Haie! Io," (you have read this in his poems). He seems instinctively to have snapped back into everyday existence. He drags me out of the shadows.

March 8

Now, no one will understand this. They swarm out of their burrows, "But you must write about him." But what I write, they don't like. Erich [Heydt][3] calls them *Ameisen,* I'm not quite sure of this, but of course it's "ants" in my little dictionary. Erich says he wants the ants or *Ameisen* to write a commentary on the *Cantos.* There are selections from them in a new German-English edition that he got in Zürich. "Do you want it?" he said and handed me the paperbook. The face looked out at me from the dark reflection of the paperbook cover. I liked the feel of the cover. The face, full-face, bronze against the dark background, looked at me, a reflection in a metal mirror. "No,"

I said and handed the book back. "But there is about you," said Erich, "here; Eva Hesse says that he invented the Imagist title of *Formel*[4] to explain the verses of the young poet—poetess—here—you." But I did not take the book. "I read that somewhere before," I said. Is this a reprint and not new, of the book I had, maybe three years ago? I had many of the books and stacks of papers and pamphlets but I sent most of them back to Vevey, to be stored with my other books in a friend's house. I read the *Cantos* or read at them or in them. Norman Pearson kept asking me to explain references. I gave it all up. Then I read an article, "Weekend with Ezra Pound,"[5] and it all came back. I asked Joan [Waluga] to get me the new edition of the old book in Zürich.

There is the Wyndham Lewis Tate Gallery portrait in the "Weekend" by David Rattray, in *The Nation* of November 16, 1957. Wyndham Lewis used to come to our little flat in Kensington to borrow Richard Aldington's razor. This annoyed Richard. Ezra and Dorothy had a slightly larger flat across the narrow hall. I found the door open one day before they were married, and Ezra there. "What—what are you doing?" I asked. He said he was looking for a place where he could fence with Yeats. I was rather taken aback when they actually moved in. It was so near. But we went soon after to Hampstead, to a larger flat that a friend had found us.

After that we did not see much of Ezra and the Kensington group, Olivia Shakespear (Dorothy's mother), Violet Hunt, Ford Madox Hueffer (as he then was) and the rest of them. The 1914 war had begun. Richard and I were married in October 1913 after what Ezra called our "unofficial honeymoon in Italy."

I saw Ezra, on the way back from Capri-Naples, in Venice that year.

He must show me a church. We darted in and out of

alleys or *calles,* across bridges, narrow passageways, the labyrinth. He was "tracing / the lay-out for the Labyrinth," from the Ramon Guthrie poem[6] [on Pound, in the same issue of *The Nation*]. It was very hot,—May, I think. The church was cool, with a balcony of icy mermaids, Santa Maria dei Miracoli. Years afterwards, I went again and I carried the votive card of Santa Maria that the sacristan had given me, in my handbag, with another (St. Mark's) token picture, during the [World] War II years in London. Ezra was in Rapallo, as we all know.

When I came here to Küsnacht, May 1946, after the war, I cleared out the grubby contents of my bag. Why did I tear up the pictures? Well, they were frayed and old, as I was, and I must find new talismans. I found them in my writing. I wrote feverishly, but the real content of my Ezra story was not touched on or only brushed in lightly.

Mr. Morley, one of the guests here, asked me if I knew Gaudier-Brzeska[7]—or he said, a Polish sculptor in London who was killed in the first war. How did we come to talk at all? I have coffee downstairs in the dining room, the days that Dr. Heydt doesn't come in. I had never mentioned Ezra, except to Heydt and Joan—now some door opens. Mr. Morley knew about him.

Mr. Morley is a tall, depressed American abstract artist, with a pleasant voice. He talked of Joyce, Yeats, Eliot. All this world, these people, come into consciousness. Today, he brings me a picture. "You must keep it," he said. It is a blue animal, lion, padding behind symbolic bars that might be trees. It is "The Poet in the Iron Cage" (*"Der Dichter im Eisernen Käfig"*). The design is hypnotizing. Joan said that she would fasten up the picture for me and came upstairs to find a place for it.

I am anonymous here or try to be. But talking and thinking of Ezra creates a human, humanizing bond. But this has only happened lately; I mean this simple, natural approach has come to me since reading and re-reading the "Weekend."

March 9

Joan looked and looked at the picture when we had our usual, ritual glass of Chianti before dinner. She had tacked it on the wall above the Lausanne bookcases that Bryher had had sent over for me. I see the lion from my bed as I write here, after breakfast. Joan said, "It looks like a water buffalo." She said, "There are birds—now, I see another bird." I don't see the lion's head from here, this might be a Minotaur. He seems to burst *out* of his cage. It is again, "stalking, pacing / as done by jaguar or ounce / in Zagreus' days," from the Guthrie poem.

The bars are trees now. Will the lion devour me or redeem me—or both?

They say I must go into Zürich for another X-ray. This terrifies me. This is the terror one can not speak of, *that walketh by night.* They might ask me to stay in the Klinik[8] again. It is the fear of being caught, caged, confined—*a confinement.* I had sixteen weeks there, in the Klinik Hirslanden, last winter. But I can walk around the house now. It is too bitter cold to go out, anyway. . . .

I did not see him at the time of my first confinement, 1915. I lost that child. The second was four years later, 1919. He hurtles himself into the decorous St. Faith's Nursing Home, in Ealing, near London. Beard, black soft hat, ebony stick—something unbelievably operatic—directoire overcoat, Verdi. He stalked and stamped the length of the room. He coughed, choked or laughed, "You look like old Mrs. Grumpy" (or some such) "in Wyncote." Wyncote was where the Pounds had lived, outside Philadelphia. True, I wore a becoming (I thought) black lace cap. Naturally, I looked no sylph. He seemed to beat with the ebony stick like a baton. I can't remember. Then, there is a sense of his pounding, pounding (*Pounding*) with the stick against the wall. He had banged that way, with a stick once before, in a taxi, at a grave crisis in my life. This was a grave crisis in my life. It was happening here. "But," he said, "my only real criticism is that this is not my child."

I wondered who had let him in. I did not know he was coming. From me, screams were inhibited, prohibitive. Did I want to scream? I was sorry that my appearance shocked him. The next day at noon, March 31, 1919, the child was born.

The first time, in the taxi, was before I was married. Frances Gregg[9] had filled the gap in my Philadelphia life after Ezra was gone, after our "engagement" was broken. Maybe the loss of Ezra left a vacuum; anyway, Frances filled it like a blue flame. I made my first trip to Europe with her and her mother, summer 1911. Frances wrote, about a year after her return to America, that she was getting married ("When this letter reaches you, I shall be married.") She said that one of the objects of her marriage to this English University Extension lecturer—or in fact the chief object—was a return to Europe so that she could join me; we would all go to Belgium together where "Louis" was lecturing.

I found Ezra waiting for me on the pavement outside the house, off Oxford Circus, where I had a room. His appearance was again unexpected, unpredictable. He began, "I as your nearest male relation . . . ," and hailed a taxi. He pushed me in. He banged with his stick, pounding (*Pounding*), as I have said. "You are not going with them." I had seen them the day before at their hotel, off Victoria Station. It was all arranged. Ezra must have seen them afterwards. "There is a vague chance that the Egg," (he called her), "may be happy. You will spoil everything." Awkwardly, at Victoria Station, I explained to a married Frances, with a long tulle travelling veil, that I wasn't coming. I had changed my mind. Awkwardly, the husband handed me back the cheque that I had made out for my ticket. Glowering and savage, Ezra waited till the train pulled out.

March 10

It was Richard Aldington[10] from Sury-en-Vaux, France, who sent me the "Weekend" article. I returned it, then asked to have it back again. I wanted Erich Heydt to read it, and Bryher,[11] and George Plank who was here for a few days. I had said to George, "It was the first time that I *laughed* about Ezra, for—how many years? It was the jam-jar or peanut-butter jar with tea." I got the article again, posted it to George in Sussex, he returned it, Joan read it. Bryher read it. Erich read it. We all felt that Ezra's surroundings were deplorable. So I talked about Ezra. Again I wrote Richard in France, asking if I should return the "Weekend." He wrote back, "Do by all means keep the Rattray article on Ezra. It is such a welcome change to have him reported as a human being, and not as journalist's abstraction or political 'cause.' "

There is a human Ezra flinging books from a table in May Sinclair's[12] studio on to an inaccessible shelf that ran under the high sloping roof. "People *impose* on you," he said, "you can't get those books down. You can't write letters to all those people." He explained to us afterwards, "It's her *Divine Fire*. You read it?" This was a swarm of minnows, according to Ezra, poets in the manner of the underprivileged hero of *The Divine Fire*. I had read the novel in America, before I left with Frances and her mother. I had never expected to meet any of these famous people. The strange thing is that Ezra was so inexpressibly kind to anyone who he felt had the faintest spark of submerged talent. I still think of those books, slim volumes of verse, first books I should imagine for the most part. No doubt Miss Sinclair summoned a janitor, a window-cleaner or a fireman with an imposing ladder. She wouldn't, with her amazing Edwardian courtesy, neglect her minnows.

Richard and Ezra and I were walking together in Kensington that morning when Ezra said, "We'll look in on May." Miss Sinclair opened the studio apartment door. Her somewhat Queen Mary bang or fringe was done up in curl papers. I tugged at Richard's sleeve to suggest that we go home, but Ezra had already swung on into the studio. May Sinclair made no reference to her early morning appearance. She was as Norman Douglas once said, "a rare thing nowadays, my dear, a gentlewoman."

March 11

I saw her alone in the early Twenties at her St. John's Wood house, and once more at my flat in Sloane Street. She then had a rather grim nurse in attendance. Soon after, she disappeared into a mental home, it was reported. I did not see her again. After her death, when I was in Lausanne, 1947, I had a notice from her lawyer. She had left 50 or 100 pounds each, to Ezra, Richard and myself, and a choice of some 50 books from her library. A long printed list was sent. The lawyer, a nephew, I think, said that there were a number of claimants for the books and suggested that I did not take too many. I asked for all of Ezra's books, Richard's, my own, several of May's novels and a Shakespeare concordance.

Wyndham Lewis died a few years ago. He was blind for some time before his death.

Was I blind? Erich Heydt, the young German *Oberarzt*

here, seemed to think so. When I came, the second time, summer 1953, after an operation in Lausanne, he jabbed an injection needle into my arm. It was perhaps the second or third time that I had seen him—or was it the first? He said, "You know Ezra Pound, don't you?" This was a shock coming from a stranger. Perhaps he injected me or re-injected me with Ezra. I managed a vague affirmative, wondering what business this was of Doctor Heydt. It appears that he had been in America on a sort of scholarship or travelling fellowship. He had visited various hospitals and clinics; among others, he had stayed for a time at St. Elizabeth's. How did he know that I knew Ezra? He had seen him in the garden, surrounded by a circle of visitors, disciples. "I asked who they were. I had seen some of them in the canteen." I did not want to talk of this. "Why don't you look at me?" said Dr. Heydt. "Why do you look out of the window. I am talking to you."

I was too weak to care or listen to what he said. But maybe I did care.

Erich Heydt got me to read some of this record to him this afternoon. He said, "The simplicity is wonderful in face of the confusion." Pedantically, he questioned my phrasing of the Eva Hesse, "She says it was to put you in the right light—*ins rechte Licht*—that he founded the *imagistische Schule*."

Séraphita.[13] A story by Balzac. The Being, he-her, disappears or dies in the snow. Séraphitus. Ezra brought me the story.

The perfection of the fiery moment can not be sustained —or can it?

March 12

There is a prayer, the *10ème Jour lunaire*.[14] It ends with the words: *Que mon coeur soit sincère en Tes statuts, afin que je ne sois par vêtu de confusion.*

I was clothed with confusion. I had been forced into the wrong groove. Is every groove wrong? I resented the years preparing for college that might have been spent with music, drawing. Poetry? Well, I had read enough poetry. "You are a poem, though your poem's naught," quoted Ezra. From what? I did not ask him. We had climbed up into the big maple tree in our garden, outside Philadelphia.

There was a crow's nest that my younger brother had built—bench boards and a sort of platform. The house is hidden by the great branches. There is an occasional cart or carriage from the highway or turnpike, beyond the hedge. At half-hour intervals, a tram or trolley jolts past. He must not miss the last "car" and the train to Wyncote, on the Main Line. "There is another trolley in a half hour," I say, preparing to slide out of the crow's nest.

"No, Dryad," he says. He snatches me back. We sway with the wind. There is no wind. We sway with the stars. They are not far.

We slide, slip, fly down through the branches, leap together to the ground. "No," I say, breaking from his arms, "No," drawing back from his kisses. "I'll run ahead and stop the trolley, no—quick, get your things—books—whatever you left in the hall." "I'll get them next time," he says. "Run," I say, "run." He just catches the trolley, swaying dangerously, barely stopping, only half stopping. Now, I must face them in the house.

"He was late again." My father was winding the clock. My mother said, "Where were you? I was calling. Didn't you hear me? Where is Ezra Pound?" I said, "O—he's gone." "Books? Hat?" "He'll get them next time." Why had I ever come down out of that tree?

". . . profile of a *Raubkatze*"—*Merkur,* January 1958,[15] an article by Peter Demetz—"beating through the air with his racket. I saw the Chinese amulet on his chest—I saw the split, celluloid eye-shade, glued together with a piece of sticking plaster . . . casually, carelessly—outside, between two huge trees—Mrs. Pound was just coming out of the old Ford. I was arranging a few garden chairs, waiting . . . mad men were around me, pop-eyed. Pound talked of his friends in Paris and it began to rain. Pound opened the door of the old Ford . . . books, laundry that Mrs. Pound had brought him, packages, jam jars, etc. He explained *Pisan Cantos*—drew plan of Pisan camp—drumming of rain—mended eye-shade—memories of a Capanius (kapaneus?)—later, talk of escape. He is the youngest, most bitter among the Grand Old Men of letters—was hiding a secret humility. . . ."

"Der Dichter im Eisernen Käfig" appeared about two years ago. Pound's love and hate is stressed in this new German *Merkur* article.

I scratched down these few careless phrases as Erich read the article to me. No doubt it is an excellent summary like many that I have read about Ezra, but it leaves me with a terrible sense of frustration. There is so much *writing* and good writing about the controversial *Dichter*. What is my contribution? I hope that Erich is right when he says of my own record or recording, "The simplicity is wonderful in face of the confusion."

March 13

For the *15ème Jour lunaire*,[16] there is a prayer . . . *ne me rends point confus dans mon espérance.*

There is the first book, sent from Venice, *A Lume Spento* [1908]. It is dedicated to William Brooke Smith. Ezra had brought him to see me. He was an art student, tall, graceful, dark, with a "butterfly bow" tie, such as is seen in the early Yeats portraits. Ezra read me a letter he wrote; this is under the lamp at our sitting-room table. The letter was poetic, effusive, written, it appeared, with a careful spacing of lines and unextravagant margin. I only glimpsed the writing, Ezra did not hand the letter to me. The boy was consumptive. His sister had just died.

He waved to us from the car once. I wondered what he was doing on our West Chester turnpike. It seemed his sister was buried near West Chester. It seemed far from Wyncote. Or do I dream this?

"What is it? What is it?" They would never answer directly. They would say, "He is so eccentric." "What is it?" "He is impossible; he told Professor Schelling that Bernard Shaw was more important than Shakespeare." "What is it?" "He makes himself conspicuous; he wore lurid, bright socks that the older students ruled out for freshmen. The sophomores threw him in the lily pond. They called him 'Lily' Pound." "What is it?" He's taking graduate courses now; that happened, if it happened, long ago. Why do the faculty ladies concern themselves with such small matters? What is it? He's gone far enough away now, as an instructor in Romance languages. *What is it?* He came back he came back, he came back.

They asked him to leave.[17] My father said, "Mr. Pound, I don't say there was anything wrong *this time*. I will not forbid you the house, but I will ask you not to come so often." *What is it?* "I found her in the snow, when I went to post a letter. She was stranded from a travelling variety company. She had nowhere to go. I asked her to my room. She slept in my bed. I slept on the floor." "What is it? There is more to it than that. Cousin Edd knows people in Wyncote who told him—." But they did not tell me what it was they told him. "What is it? Cousin Edd knows some people in Wyncote—." "O—*that*—and I had thought that our Cousin Edd was a decent old chap." A clergyman, a cousin of my mother's, had told her—"What? what? what?"

"They say in Wyncote that I am bi-sexual and given to unnatural lust." I did not understand the implication of the words. Nowadays any sophisticated teenager would laugh at them. But this is—1906? 1907?

"You must come away with me, Dryad." "How can I? How can I?" His father would scrape up enough for him to live on. I had nothing. "Anyway," an old school friend confided, as if to cheer me up, "they say that he was engaged to Mary Moore, anyhow. Bessie Elliot could have had him for the asking. There was Louise Skidmore, before that." *What is it? What is it?* The engagement, such as it was, was shattered like a Venetian glass goblet, flung on the floor.

Erich said, when I read this last section to him, this afternoon, "But you did not say you were actually engaged." "It's implied. I didn't read all the pages to you. I did read the section about Frances filling a gap in my life, after the engagement was broken. Anyway, would she, this—the period Miss of our narrative, have gone on with the fiery kisses that I speak of, in the beginning, unless there had been—had been—at least, an understanding?" "You didn't say he gave you a ring. Did he give you a ring?" "Of course—how *German* you are—." "It was announced, everyone knew it?" "O, how you get hold of the unimportant details. Yes, no. I mean, it was understood but my parents were unhappy about it and I was shy and frightened. I didn't have the usual conventional party—lunch, dinner or announcement dance, if that is what you mean. But *what* does it matter?"

"His parents came to see you?" "Of course." "They were pleased?" "Very—mine weren't, as I say. Mrs. Pound

· 1 5 ·

brought me an exquisite pearl pendant." "Then, you *were* engaged. Did you give the ring back?" "Of course." "Did he write to you when he went to Venice?" "Yes—yes—yes—yes—yes—."

March 14

"What did your father mean by 'I don't say there was anything wrong *this time?*' Did he know about it? How did he know about it? You don't say how he knew about it." "Good Lord—it's implied—there was talk—." "Who talked? What did they say?" "How could I know." "Didn't you ask?" "No—no—no—no—."

"Was this a Quaker college? Was it far from Philadelphia?" "I don't think Quaker—Middle West somewhere—not very near—." "It must have been very hard for you in a family like that. Were you jealous of this girl he found who slept in his bed?"

"How could I be jealous of anyone who slept in his bed?" "Then you didn't—?" "Do you expect me to go into biological, pathological details?" "Yes." "But why?" "Because it's interesting and because I always knew there was something you wouldn't tell me."

"Were you there when your father told him not to come again?" "Yes—but he said not to come so often." "Did he come?" "Yes—no—stop—my half-brother and sister-in-law lived in a wing of the house. It was a large house. We met there—sometimes in a friend's house—." "Well, tell me—."

"The next time, maybe; Monday, maybe." "I could come sooner." "No, we arranged the four days. No, it's five o'clock. You'll miss your train—." "I ordered the taxi." "Well, anyhow, it's five o'clock—you have your next session. . . ."

Session? He called our meetings, our visits, tea sessions. He comes three or four times a week. He has his own studio apartment in Zürich now, where he sees his analysands and patients. I went there a number of times, summer before last, but nothing "happened." Did he expect, did I expect, anything to "happen"?

The years were immaterial. He liked my light summer dresses. Ezra was not consciously a love-image. But perhaps he lurked there, hid there, under the years. In making me feel young and happy, Erich prodded him out.

We were curled up together in an armchair when my father found us. I was "gone." I wasn't there. I disentangled myself. I stood up; Ezra stood beside me. It seems we must have swayed, trembling. But I don't think we did. "Mr. Pound, I don't say there was anything wrong. . . ." Mr. Pound, it was all wrong. You turn into a Satyr, a Lynx, and the girl in your arms (Dryad, you called her), for all her fragile, not yet lost virginity, is *Maenad, bassarid*.[18] God keep us from Canto LXXIX, one of the *Pisan Cantos*.

Mr. Pound, with your magic, your "strange spells of old deity,"[19] why didn't you complete the metamorphosis? Pad, pad, pad, . . . come along, my Lynx. Let's get out of here. You are suffocating and I am hungry. You spoke of grapes somewhere—you were starving.

March 15

"What did you feel when this—this Walter told you that?" "Look—it's impossible to say. I felt bleak, a chasm opened—." "But you said that you had loved this American girl, this Frances—and you were going around with Richard—." "I don't know what I felt. I had met Walter years before, in America, in a house the Pounds had for the summer. Ezra had come back from Europe. He asked Frances and me to this house to hear Walter play. Ezra had had a grand piano sent out from Philadelphia. 'O,' Ezra said, 'they said, *"Walter Rummel"*—and anything was had for the asking." "A concert pianist?" "Yes." "An American?" "His grandfather was the Morse-Code Morse. His name was Walter Morse Rummel. His father was a German. Mrs. Shakespear was very fond of him at one time. Richard and I had seen a good deal of him in Paris." "You were married then?" "No."

"You mean, Ezra told people that you were engaged to him?" "I don't know—only Walter said, 'I think I ought to tell you, though I promised Mrs. Shakespear not to,— don't let her know or anyone. But there is an understanding. Ezra is to marry Dorothy Shakespear.[20] He shouldn't tell other people or imply to other people that he—that you—.' " "Did you speak to Ezra of this?" "No."

"What exactly did he say to people?" "O—I don't know. . . ." Drifting. Drifting. Meeting with him alone or with others at the Museum tea room. We all read in the British Museum reading room. Dark walls and statues that looked dingy. Frances had gone home. I could wait till my parents came. My father, at 70, had retired from the University. My mother wrote, "We could meet in Genoa." I had my own allowance now. Drifting? "But Dryad," (in the Museum tea room), "this is poetry." He slashed with a pencil. "Cut this out, shorten this line. 'Hermes of the Ways' is a good title. I'll send this to Harriet Monroe of *Poetry*. Have you a copy? Yes? Then we can send this, or I'll type it when I get back. Will this do?" And he scrawled "H.D. Imagiste" at the bottom of the page.

I was hiding. There was the heroic sequence, those last years in London. "What is it you are hiding?" Erich Heydt insisted. I was hiding myself and Ezra, standing before my father, caught "in the very act" you might say. For no "act" afterwards, though biologically fulfilled, had had the significance of the first *demi-vierge* embraces. The significance of "first love" can not be overestimated. If the "first love" is an uncoordinated entity, Angel-Devil—or Angel-Daemon or Daimon, Séraphitus-Séraphita—what then? Find a coordinated convention, Man-Hero who will compensate, complete the picture. By what miracle does the *mariage du ciel et de la terre* find consummation? It filled my fantasies and dreams, my prose and poetry for ten years. But in the end, intellectual and physical perfection, the laurel wreath of the acclaimed achievement must be tempered, balanced, re-lived, re-focused or even sustained by the unpredictable, the inchoate, challenged by a myth, a legend—the poet (Vidal, shall we say), changed to Wolf or Panther, hunted down and captured.

> There is a stir of dust from old leaves
> Will you trade roses for acorns . . .[21]

March 16

"Goodbye Dave, you'll come over Christmas Day, won't you?" This "Weekend with Ezra Pound" by Rattray seems to me the first human personal presentation of Ezra that I have seen. True, I had lost touch, was "hiding," but I had newspapers and periodicals showered on me during the years. The German was too difficult but I felt they cared—but was that a political dodge? I asked a young German whom I met when Erich Heydt had his apartment here in *Geduld*. The boy said, "No—we read him for himself, in East and in West Germany." Still, I was not satisfied.

Erich said, "I was disappointed that Ezra did not give your address to the Ratt—." "Don't call him the Ratt—but maybe Ratt doesn't mean *rat* in your language." "It's easier, than *Ratt*-ray—*doch, doch*—he gave Richard's name, anyhow, though he said not to mention E.P. to him, 'just be the *jeune homme modeste*.' Why doesn't he mention you?" "He must know that I don't see many people—." "But it says the *Ratt*-ray is in Europe, a Fulbright scholar in France. He could come to Zürich. Or are you afraid that he might make fun of you? Of us? What did they think, the girl with the double chin, the double chins, sketching, and the boy with the coarse features, and the one with a face, slippery as if modelled in soap?" "You seem to know the article by heart." "Wouldn't these visitors be hurt? The girl, for instance—he said he thought when he first saw her, that she was a patient from another ward."

Just now, hearing *Solveigslied* on my radio, I am reminded of how Ezra took me to see Richard Mansfield's *Peer Gynt* in Philadelphia. Solveig—Penelope—spinning, weaving. I couldn't remember how the story ended. I remembered the button-molder and Peer's escape. He wasn't melted down again into an unrecognizable nonentity. He remained an entity, he is recognizable. Mad? He always was eccentric. "O, Ezra Pound's crazy," was the verdict of my schoolgirl contemporaries. "He wanted them to throw him in the pond." So the story was going around from the beginning, but I forgot it till it cropped up again after the incident that had lost him his job. Spinning? Weaving? Then, I remembered the end of the play, an ancient Solveig in a white wig, a decrepit Peer Gynt in a white wig, meet in the doorway of the original Solveig cottage, on the edge of a picturesque pasteboard forest. No, this is something different.

Dr. Erich Heydt injected me with Ezra, jabbing a needle into my arm, "You know Ezra Pound, don't you?" This was almost five years ago. It took a long time for the virus or the anti-virus to take effect. But the hypodermic needle did its work or didn't it? There was an incalculable element. There was something. To say nothing "happened" in Heydt's studio apartment is to put it very crudely. "Tired? Rest on the couch—." "No." The very idea of a studio couch and tenderness brought with it a *cloud,* not a *crowd* of memories. "Why don't you tell me?" "I'm always telling you." "Yes—but you're hiding something."

"What is it? What is it?" We were running to catch the train. "But what does it matter if you miss it—you can take the next one—." I had stopped suddenly, leaning against a wall, gesturing as for a taxi. He caught my wrist, "There's plenty of time. You're hysterical. Something's upset you—." "It reminds me, running along a town street—a town—Philadelphia—." "You've something there but you won't tell me—." "I can't tell you. I don't know what it is." Room is made for us—but only just—on the end of a crowded station bench. He took my hands in his. "Must you hold my hands like this?" "Yes." The crowd surged around us. "There's sure to be someone from Küsnacht— to report Herr Doktor Heydt and Madame A., huddled on a bench together." No. There was no one from anywhere, we were enclosed in another dimension. A small male child with short red-gold curls poked into the market basket of the woman beside us. Where did he come from? How did he get there? It is only a moment. The inevitable parent emerges, moving against the crowd. Parent? Guardian? He is tall and gaunt. I can not take it in. He isn't there or I am not there but the market basket is adequately materialized and the typical *Hausfrau* beside us on the station bench. "I'm sorry, I said you were hysterical. I was just worried." The train was rumbling nearer. "Should you go back?" "No—I shouldn't." But I pushed forward with the crowd. "Tomorrow?" he calls up to the open window of the moving train.

March 17

Erich asked me if my parents liked his parents. "They only met a few times but yes—yes," I said, "in a purely conventional way. Mrs. Pound was a beautiful woman, well-bred, somewhat affected in manner. One was inclined to be embarrassed and baffled by her little witticisms, her epigrams, as one so often was by Ezra's. Mr. Pound was hearty, informal, very kind. He was a government assayer at the Philadelphia Mint. He invited a group of us to visit the inner sanctum. He showed us minute weights and measures, explained superficially the analysis of the gold—*"There,"* and he unlocked a heavy door—it seems it was a door to an iron-bound cupboard, rather than a safe; anyway, there were stacks of gold bars—*"Here,"* and coins were piled in neat rows, "will you help yourself," chuckling heartily.

Has anyone ever noted, reported this, or even known this? It seems to me that Homer Pound's government job in Philadelphia played an extravagant part in Ezra's later compulsions. Usury? *Usura.* Ezra was at one time, it seems, obsessed with this word. I followed these *Canto* references with difficulty. I don't mean that Ezra wanted the gold for himself. He wanted to change the world with it. Can one change the world with it?

> Gold on her head, and gold on her feet,
> And gold where the hems of her kirtle meet,
> And a golden girdle round my sweet;
>   *Ah! qu'elle est belle, La Marguerite.*

He read me William Morris in an orchard under blossoming—yes, they must have been blossoming—apple trees.

March 18

It was Ezra who really introduced me to William Morris. He literally shouted "The Gilliflower of Gold" in the

orchard. How did it go? *Hah! hah! la belle jaune giroflée.*
And there was "Two Red Roses across the Moon" and
"The Defence of Guenevere." It was at this time that he
brought me the *Séraphita* and a volume of Swedenborg—
Heaven and Hell? Or is that Blake? He brought me volumes of Ibsen and of Bernard Shaw. He brought me
Whistler's *Ten O'Clock.* He scratched a gadfly, in imita-
tion of Whistler's butterfly, as a sort of signature in his
books at that time. He was a composite James McNeill
Whistler, Peer Gynt and the victorious and defeated he-
roes of the William Morris poems and stories. He read
me "The Haystack in the Floods" with passionate emotion.

He brought me the Portland, Maine, Thomas Mosher
reprint of the Iseult and Tristram story.[22] He called me
Is-hilda and wrote a sonnet a day; he bound them in a
parchment folder. There was a series of Yogi books, too.

Actually, the gadfly hieroglyph was suggested by a book
of that name. I do not know who wrote *The Gadfly.*[23] It
was a novel about Italian patriots or partisans, as we now
call them, or some *Risorgimento* incident. The word
"zany" came in. I have never seen it before. The hero gets
mixed up with some travelling actors—or fair or circus?
I don't remember. Disguise? Escape? It is a bitter, tragic
hero, this *Gadfly.* Does the story predict or foreshadow the
last episodes and the Pisan legend?

Joan just came in for my letters; to my surprise, she
remembers *The Gadfly*—"Rather before my time, mother
had it." She found the author, Ethel Voynich, in my *Reader's Encyclopedia.* She does not remember any circus or
fair, but she has the same impression that I have of some
grim, involved, political tragedy.

I see from Eva Hesse's note in the German-English *Ezra
Pound, Dichtung und Prosa*[24] that it is Wabash College,

Indiana, that was the scene of "this girl he found" that Erich spoke of. "Were you jealous of this girl he found who slept in his bed?" Ezra was only four months there. But I must have addressed a good many letters to Wabash College, Crawfordsville, Indiana. I confused it with Hamilton College, Clinton, New York, where he was a student for two years. Is this important?

It perhaps helps to clarify the *cloud* of memories. It is the emotional content that matters. I wrote, "The perfection of the fiery moment can not be sustained—or can it?" Erich says of himself that he is the *Spiegel,* the mirror, the burning-glass that "catches the light all round." Yes, he gets the situation *ins rechte Licht,* but I can not explain to him how painful it is to me at times to retain the memory of the "fiery moment."

Maybe Erich catches it in the *Spiegel*—but he has only to reflect it. I have to substantiate it.

March 19

I am walking on air, though I can hardly walk at all, due to a regrettable bone fracture. Over a year ago, I slipped on a small rug on an overwaxed, highly polished floor. Ezra wrote, " 'ow did you 'appen to step on that thar soap"—or something of that sort. He kept writing, urging me to do some Greek translations. I found his letters almost indecipherable or untranslatable—and this made me and Richard Aldington too, to whom he was writing at the time, very sad. But the "actual" Ezra only manifested with the reading and re-reading of the "Weekend." And now Joan has discovered a *cache* of his books, behind other books in my cupboard. So now we find the original *Dichtung und Prosa,* pencilled by Erich Heydt, 1954, in the H.D. and Imagist section.

The original lot of the early books must still be in Lon-

BALLAD OF THE SON'S HUNTING

I hang from the horn of the crescent moon
    To watch the sun out-ride .
He 's a-riding o' the boundries
    By creation 's t'other side .

I left myself a-weeping
    For a love that would not smile .
My soul hath rode a hunting
    With the star dogs for a while .

I hang from the horn of the crescent moon
    To watch the hunt out-ride .
There rings shrill cry and horning
    From creation 's t'other side .

My soul hath caught the sun out-riding
    By creation 's t'other side .
The sun hath kissed her lips out-right
    And hath my soul to bride .

Ezra Pound , Milligan Place , Crawfordsville , Ind .

Facsimile of early manuscript poem with Ezra Pound's
"gadfly" signature

don or with my friend Bryher in Vaud, but there is a ripe
crop here; a huge *Cantos* volume, *Rock Drill,* American
and English editions of *Confucius,* the *Sophokles*
[*Women of Trachis*] and several of the beautiful little
English-Italian books of the Pesce d'Oro, Milan, sent me
by Mary de Rachewiltz.

"Why are you so excited when you read these notes to
me?" said Erich this afternoon. "I don't know—I don't
know—it's the *fiery moment* but it's all so long ago." "It
has no time," said Erich, "it's the existentialist" (word
that I can never cope with) "moment. It has no time, it's
out of time, eternal."

March 21

I was baffled, puzzled, bewildered. I see references, in
"Weekend," to certain *Canto* omissions or black-outs. I
must check on this. It is difficult to check up on separate
sections, without becoming entangled in the whole. Soon
after seeing some of these original or early *Canto* varia-
tions, in the Pounds' Holland Place apartment in Kensington, opposite our own flat, we moved. Black-out. Just a
memory of a shock at the look, the lines, the words on the
newly printed pages that Ezra showed us. Mrs. Shakespear's brother said, "Why must he write about things
that we all do every day and don't talk about."

Chthonian darkness—the black-out. I don't pretend to
understand. We have gone through some Hell together,
separately.

March 22

Am I mad then, or is he? I could not answer the question but handed the letter to Dr. Heydt to read. This was
in the beginning when I did not know Erich Heydt so
well. He laughed at the letter—"What does he mean by
telling you to crawl out of your pig stye?"[25] I didn't know

what Ezra meant. I don't know now. I read in *Motive and Method*[26] today of various *Canto* references to Circe. In time, I will look them up.

March 23

Piere Vidal, the troubadour of whom I have spoken, "dressed in wolf-skins for the love of Lady Loba de Peugnautier (whose name means wolf). . . ." I quote Sister M. Bernetta Quinn, O.S.F., from her contribution to the series of essays on the *Cantos, Motive and Method.* Sister Bernetta refers to this madness as "lycanthropy." I follow her exposition, "The Metamorphoses of Ezra Pound," with admiration and respect. Myself, I have so far, felt too involved in the legend to judge fairly, or rather to see clearly.

I see, but perhaps not clearly, the poet appropriating the attributes of the famous founder of Rome—or rather of the legendary Wolf (Lupus or Lupa) who rescued and saved that founder. Is our Pard or Panther a Savior, a Lover rather than an outlaw, an iconoclast? Was it love of the incomparable "Lady Loba" that lured him to Radio Rome and that in the end, was his undoing? But no and yes. He is far from lost. He is centralized and accessible. A thousand *Ameisen,* ant hill upon ant hill of provincial colleges, have had a curious insemination. Has this ever happened in the history of America or anywhere?

Lycanthropy, a kind of madness in which the patient fancies himself to be a wolf; Lycanthrope, a wolf-man; wolf, Greek *lykos*—I read in my Chambers dictionary. The word *lykos,* as a word, recalls the Lynx, so poignantly invoked in the famous section of the Pisan Canto LXXIX.

March 24

Then Frobenius;[27] another mystery is partly solved in *Motive and Method* in an essay, "Pound and Frobenius" by Guy Davenport. Ezra kept writing me to get Frobenius. It was when I was in Lausanne, soon after Ezra was installed in St. Elizabeth's. No bookshop had Frobenius and they seemed never to have heard of him. I imagined Frobenius as a Swede, a mystic, perhaps unconsciously relating him to Swedenborg and the early books that Ezra brought me. It turned out, after a number of letters between us, that he wanted me to get Frobenius for myself, not to send to him, as I had at first imagined. Now, I find that Frobenius was a sort of *Kultur* archeologist and that Ezra had at one time made a sort of Odysseus-Pound alterego of him. Frobenius had a connection with Frankfurt but of "incredible obscurity," to use the phrase of the author of this essay. Ezra Pound and Carl Jung, the author states, were the chief enthusiasts for Frobenius' work on primitive cultures.

We find oddly, then, another clue to Ezra's divided loyalties. If Italy is the "Lady Loba," the Lupa mother-symbol, is not Germany by way of Frobenius (the Odysseus of Ezra's fantasy) the giant father? Of course, we need not remind our readers, if we ever have any, that his father's name was Homer.

These clues that I personally find so fascinating are jeered at by the supersophisticated. I painfully got together some notes in this *naïf* manner after being urged and urged to pay some tribute to the "Maestro" for a birthday (65?). The short article was judged "not suitable" but was not even returned to me.[28]

March 25

There is the incident of the "Hilda Book." I heard it was up for sale or had been sold. Is this a forgery or is it the *Is-hilda* set of poems that Ezra bound together in a parchment cover and gave me? Erich was very angry about the article. "You had no copy? But I thought you always made copies. Surely, this is a theft, a crime. Can you not get a lawyer to see to it? Why didn't you at the time—and the 'Hilda Book'—," of which I had just told him.

I explained to Erich that I had been busy then, in Lausanne and Lugano, on my prose and poetry, dealing with, or directly or indirectly inspired by, the dramatic war years in London. I was annoyed, no doubt emotionally shaken at the thought of the "Hilda Book," for the only possible clue that I could imagine to its appropriation was by way of Frances, of whom I have written. She was killed with her mother and daughter in the Plymouth Blitz. A friend of hers had written me of it and of certain of his own books that were found. But I knew that Andrew [Gibson] would have been the first to tell me of this book, which possibly I might have given to Frances, so very long ago, after parting with Ezra.

March 26

"Was Andrew her husband?" Erich asked me this afternoon, when I read him this last entry. "No, no, no—Louis had faded out years and years ago. Andrew was the godfather of her son Oliver." "Where was Oliver?" "He was allegedly in the Navy, but Andrew could not trace him, and I wrote and never heard. Andrew said he thought that Oliver 'was lost from his ship,' but maybe Oliver turned up after all; maybe he found the 'Hilda Book' among his mother's relics—literally, reliques." "How strange it is, how you weave over and back; the threads hold Europe and America together."

"That is what Ezra's *Cantos* were trying to do—what they do. I must find you a beautiful *Canto* image—" and I found it and read "San Cristoforo provided transport / with a little Christo gripping his hair"[29] And this—and I

started to read from *Rock-Drill* but put the book down.
"I read too much this morning. I have only lately dared
to try to read through the *Cantos*. But just now, before
you came in, when I felt dazed and dizzy, some of my own
lines came to me and laid the ghost, as it were. I had de-
veloped along another line, in another dimension—only
the opposites could meet in the end. How funny, I remember how he said to me in London, . . . 'Let's be engaged
—don't tell . . .' well, whoever it was, not just then Dorothy." "Then you were the third in line?" "No—I was the
first—." "And he came to you in the Nursing Home, you
said, and wanted you to have his child—." "Well, wanted
the child that I was about to have to be his, to have been
his, 'My only real criticism is that this is not my child.' "

March 27

I read Canto 90, Latin, Greek, Italian and all the rest
of it, aloud to Erich, this afternoon. Did I really read all
of it? Probably, only a section. I gain a new power *over*
the material, the invocation "m'elevasti" does invoke, does
call one out "from under the rubble" of daily cares and
terrors.

I have been seeing or trying to see a whirling kaleido-
scope. *"Ubi Amor ibi oculus est."* The thought of Ezra
was part of the "rubble heap," my actual war experiences.
Nor could I follow the intricacies of the legal accusation.
My eye, following too rapidly the uneven lines of the difficult pages, was yet part of my intellectual equipment. I re-
fused to be taken in, I must see clearly. I could not *see*
clearly but I could *hear* clearly, as I read, "m'elevasti / out
of Erebus." I could at last accept the intoxication of "Ku-
thera sempiterna" and the healing of "myrrh and olibanum
on the altar stone / giving perfume."

March 30, Palm Sunday

> Le Paradis n'est pas artificiel
> > but is jagged,
> For a flash,
> > for an hour.
> Then agony,
> > then an hour,
> > > then agony, . . .

Dorothy Shakespear, Dorothy Pound, the "Weekend" article tells us, sits in a corner, "her corner," sheltered, not wishing to see or be seen. I had a letter from her yesterday, the first in many years. I keep looking for her in the *Canto* series, *Rock-Drill*. To me, she is *Leucothea,* who in the last section, *had pity* on the ship-wrecked Odysseus. She is "leukos, Leukothea / white foam, a sea-gull."

Undine,[30] in the "Weekend," is sketching D.P., as Dorothy signed herself in the letter. Undine is reported to have said, "I think she has a beautiful profile, but it is so difficult. . . ." It is indeed difficult. We don't hear enough of D.P. and her heroic fortitude, though I do not visualize her as Penelope in this special instance, but rather as that "mortal once / Who now is a sea-god."

March 31

Erich says again this afternoon when I question the exact meaning of "indicted," as used in the December 1957 number of *Poetry,*[31] in a letter to the editor about Ezra, "but why do you get so excited?" I explained that I had read in the [William Rose] Benét *Reader's Encyclopedia* that Ezra had been arrested and tried for high treason (1945), but was "judged insane." Erich thought "indicted" referred simply to the formal accusation. I don't know.

"In any case," I say to Erich, "it is good to be excited, to feel this."

My story as lived out in the second war in London might well have been that of Dorothy Shakespear; her story could not have been, but becomes in retrospect, mine. The two men, diametrically opposed, set off each other, the London "opposite number" of my life-long Isis search, and the Odysseus-Pound descended into the land of the shades in the *Pisan Cantos*. No. There is no resemblance. But I completed my own *cantos* as Norman called them, again in the Greek setting; mine is *Helen and Achilles* [*Helen in Egypt*].[32] There is resemblance in this, the two men meet in war, the Trojan War, the Achilles of my fantasy and imagination and the Odysseus of Ezra's. They do not meet, they never can meet in life. But the two women, Helen (of my creative reconstruction) and the Penelope (a human actuality) can communicate.

April 1

Erich queries my quotation from the Benét and looks up the Eva Hesse reference in *Dichtung und Prosa*, in which she states that Ezra's condition was diagnosed as *frühzeitige Senilität,* brought on by his unjust treatment in the Pisan camp. I question the *Senilität* and Erich explains that actually it is a psychological word that is sometimes used, as it is in a way less damaging or derogatory than paranoia or one of the other technical terms for madness or insanity.

It is painful to discuss this but I feel that an almost algebraic formula is necessary. I can not say that any of us are satisfied with the equation, Fascist-party-line-by-short-wave-to-America + Poet = *Senilität*. There is, as I myself felt in my "Lady Luba" or Lupe finding, the hint of the *crime passionnel,* for which (as the second letter to *Poetry,* in this same December issue, states) " 'no jury,' as the phrase has it, 'will convict.' "

The two letters are very revealing, "An Exchange on Ezra Pound." The second, by Hugh Kenner, concludes with an injunction to the "literary critic" and, it follows, to every intelligent reader of Ezra Pound. Apart from and along with the purely legal aspect, Mr. Kenner makes it quite clear that anyone who has "made himself conversant with the thought, the poetry, and the intentions has the duty of testifying as he can."

April 4, Good Friday

I had a long letter from Norman Pearson yesterday. He had seen them both. Erich has gone, for ten days, on his Easter holiday to Venice. I long to share my news with him but it must wait. Bryher is here with Sylvia Beach for Easter. Perhaps I can talk with them, as I discussed the "Weekend" with Bryher and George in the beginning, and laughed, really laughed, as I have said, for the first time, about Ezra. But Erich's is a different, "existentialist" (his word) dimension. I am trembling beside him. We are seated at the end of a crowded station bench. He has taken my hands. "Must you hold my hands?" "Yes." Into our consciousness and in our consciousness, in mine at any rate, is a small, delicate yet sturdy male object. The child reaches into the market basket of the woman on the bench beside us. His curls are short and red and gold. He is the "fiery moment" incarnate.

How many loaves and fishes are here? But we need not feed this multitude, not loaves and fishes. It is mostly apples. "Pomona, Pomona. Christo Re, Dio Sole."[33]

April 5, Easter Saturday

"But," he said, "my only real criticism is that this is not my child."

This is the child but a long time after, drawn into consciousness by Erich Heydt, stabilized, exactly visualized, one summer day on the crowded platform of the *Zürich-Stadelhofen* station.

The Child was with us when George Plank, Bryher, and I first discussed the "Weekend" and I laughed about Ezra, for the first time in the 12 years of his confinement. I heard his voice, "Goodbye Dave, you'll come over Christmas Day, won't you?" There is no *reason* to accept, to condone, to forgive, to forget what Ezra has done. Sylvia [Beach] made it very clear last night. And here, I should renounce my hope of recalling Ezra, if I dare think of Sylvia's confinement in a detention camp, her near-starvation, the meager rations shared with her by her friend Adrienne Monnier, during a term of hiding. Dare I go on? There is no *reason* to hope for his release. "He has books, everything; students come to me in Paris and tell me about him. *Fascist*. Those dreadful people he knows—that man—." "Yes," I said, "I know, news items have been sent me, but. . . ." "There is a group there. He has everything. . . ." "I know." "It was a great mistake, that official prize they gave him." I said, "But. . . ."

I said, "But." There is no argument, pro or con. You catch fire or you don't catch fire. "This fruit has a fire within it, / Pomona, Pomona. / No glass is clearer than are the globes of this flame / what sea is clearer than the pomegranate body / holding the flame? / Pomona, Pomona."

April 7, Easter Monday
So the very day I enter this last note, I hear again from Norman Pearson, "It looks more and more possible that the day of liberation may finally come." He sends *New York Times*, April 2 report, and a short article from April 3; *London Times* is sent me, and Joan found a *Jours de*

France, April 5 notice, *"Ezra Pound, le Mallarmé U. S. ne mourra pas chez les fous."* I have among my Easter letters, one too, from Mary de Rachewiltz from Schloss Brunnenburg, Tyrol, "There is some hope of having father with us soon."

April 9

Mary asked me to visit her when I was at Lugano. There was a local bus, she said, it was not far. But I never went. She sent me photographs of herself and the children. She is looking out of a window of the *Schloss* or castle, like a girl in a fairy tale, or "Sister Helen," a poem. She gazes out over the romantic Tyrol landscape, far, far. I hardly dare think of her and a copy of an early portrait that Ezra had sent me, with her hair, wheat-gold, flowing down over her shoulders. There is Sigifredo too, reaching up to a sort of della Scala knocker on a great door, with fair hair in a halo. Mary again asks me to visit them, "especially now as there is some hope of having father with us soon."

I wait for letters with the intense apprehension with which I waited almost 50 years ago, when Ezra left finally for Europe. Through the years, I have imposed or superimposed this apprehension on other people, other letters. A sort of *rigor mortis* drove me onward. No, my poetry was not dead but it was built on or around the crater of an extinct volcano. Not *rigor mortis*. No, No! The vines grow more abundantly on those volcanic slopes. Ezra would have destroyed me and the center they call "Air and Crystal" of my poetry.

Now, I am in a fever of apprehension and excitement. I was separated from my friends, my family, even from America, by Ezra. I did not analyse this. When Frances came into my life, I could talk about it—but even so, only superficially. But I read her some of the poems that Ezra and I had loved together, chiefly Swinburne. "You read so beautifully," said Frances. I read Andrew Lang's translation of Theocritus that Ezra had brought me. I wrote a poem to Frances in a Bion and Moschus mood.

> O hyacinth of the swamp-lands,
>   Blue lily of the marshes,
> How could I know,
>   Being but a foolish shepherd,
>   That you would laugh at me?

April 10

Father. In the new Eva Hesse Arche Verlag[34] edition of selections of Ezra's prose, there is a photograph of Ezra as he left the Pisan camp, fettered, between two detectives. There are the 1946–1948 pictures which are familiar from the book jackets, and the 1955 one in the deck chair in the garden at St. Elizabeth's. There is the earliest photograph, taken, they state here (and in the little booklet[35] that Mary sent me, published by Pesce d'Oro, Milan, for the 70th birthday) in Venice, at the time of the publication of his first book, *A Lume Spento,* 1908. I am sure that this picture is much earlier. The atmosphere is not Venetian—nor the chair. This is a younger Ezra even than the one I met first when I was 15.

April 11

He shakes his tawny head (wheat-colored, I have written, and Ezra has written, "a sheaf of hair / Thick like a wheat swathe"), gone grey now, they say, and the *Ameisen,* he seated on the grass, clutch eagerly for the scattered grains. Some fell by the wayside. Bushel baskets of inseminating beauty fell upon barren ground. There is much chaff among the wheat. Who can sort out the contents of the controversial *Cantos?*

April 12

Norman Pearson can sort them out. He writes me, "They are an ambitious poem and a great poem, and the problems he presents (even when I don't agree with the solutions) are the problems of our age."

I spoke of provincial colleges having had a curious insemination. But years ago, the older foundations accepted Ezra Pound. We know of his staunch supporters, Robert Frost, T. S. Eliot, Auden, Hemingway, and we have the names of that gallant band that awarded him the rabidly contested or controverted Bollingen Prize in 1949, for the *Pisan Cantos*. But my contact is with Pearson and that poignant appeal, "Tell Pearson I can't go it alone."

April 13

Pearson mentions this in one of his last letters, as "his agonized appeal." Joan finds me a notice from *Le Figaro Littéraire*, April 12, *Ezra Pound "ressuscité"?* It seems that a great deal will be resurrected or re-born once Ezra is free. Consciously or unconsciously, it seems that we have been bound with him, bound up with him and his fate.

April 14

Waiting—what news, what letters, what press cuttings? I don't suppose that I really wanted to keep his letters. There was a great untidy bundle of them, many of them written on notepaper he had appropriated from hotels, on a sort of grand tour a wealthy aunt or old family friend had taken him. There was a group photograph, tourists in costume, a young Ezra in a fez. Was that among the papers? It was as if he wrote me from those fabulous romantic places, Carcassonne, Mount St. Michael. I see the illustrations on the letter heads. The writing did not change appreciably, it scrawled as always, or was comparatively

neatly spaced, as in the *autografo* of the reproduced "Venetian Night Litany"[36] in the *Piccola Antologia* that Mary
sent me. I did not ask about the letters when I met my parents in Genoa, autumn 1912—was it? But my mother took
me aside, "I think you will be relieved to know that your
father burnt the old letters. . . ."

Erich was very shocked. Perhaps I was too, but that
shock, as with the other Poundiana, lay dormant.

Erich liked my fertility symbol, as he called it, the head,
the tawny wheat-colored hair (now gone grey), scattering
grains or seeds for the eager *Ameisen,* clustered on the
grass or crowded in the dim, uncanny hall of St. Elizabeth's. We wait with apprehension but with a new sort of
peace. This is what supremely matters. Sheath upon sheath
of self seems peeled away. I begin to understand this
"strange man" as the *London Times* of April 9 called him,
in a sympathetic special article. I was not equipped to understand the young poet.

April 15

I had letters at one time from a certain Charles [Mar-
tell], one of the St. Elizabeth's circle. He moved later to
New Jersey and I had not the heart or energy to continue
answering his strange, fascinating letters. Ezra suggested
that I send him cards or pictures. I had sent Ezra most of
my old Venice cards and some photographs of St. Mark's
mosaics. Charles wrote that Dorothy had sent him a Re-
douté rose-card (I think it was) that I had sent her. In the
last post card that I had from Charles, he spoke of seeing
Ezra again. Charles wrote, "He said you were a 'pink
moth.' " It was a line from an early poem. I don't know
where or if it was ever published, "she danced like a pink
moth in the shrubbery."[37]

I danced in the garden in the moonlight, like a mad thing. *Maenad and bassarid.* It is not necessary to understand.

April 16

Erich brought me a beautiful ruby-glass bowl from Venice. It is exactly Pomona, Pomona. "No glass is clearer than are the globes of this flame." I had not read this pomegranate section to Erich but the small cup-bowl—"no, no, not an ash-tray," I tell him—exactly materializes these lines. "This fruit has a fire within it." The small bowl is heavy with a white-blue-silver rim, one feels that it is filled with red wine. It is. "It is the Grail," I tell Erich.

A letter from Bryher says, "I heard on A[merican]-F[orces]N[etwork] this morning that they had moved to quash the indictment and release Pound . . . , but it will take a while anyhow."

April 18, Friday

Joan found me Undine's little book[38] in Zürich, with Ezra's introduction. The pictures turn on the wheel or turn the Wheel, "Undine, who is the first to show a capacity to manifest in paint, or in la ceramica what is most to be prized in my writing." This seems a return to the early D. G. Rossetti and the *Vita Nuova* translation and pre-Raphaelite pictures that Ezra brought me. Concern with "The Blessed Damozel"! Surely, Ezra read it to me—yes—and the "Dante in Verona." Undine seems myself *then.* One esteems Ezra's Gaudier-Brzeska, Wyndham Lewis, Brancusi enthusiasms. But this is something different. A hand (Ezra's?) holds a tiny ceramica head, in the first picture, called "Testa Invocatrice." All the heads in this little book are an invocation; there is "Patria" with the "Christo" and the sad "St. Elizabeth's Madonna."

April 19, Saturday

Undine seems myself *then*. I think of her when AFN, last night, at 8, says simply that Ezra Pound, the American poet is to be released. AFN concludes that he will live in Italy. But this is not 1908. Undine is a mature artist. I was 21 when Ezra left and it was some years later that he scratched "H. D. Imagiste," in London, in the Museum tea room, at the bottom of a typed sheet, now slashed with his creative pencil, "Cut this out, shorten this line."

H.D.—Hermes—Hermeticism and all the rest of it.

April 20, Sunday

The picture in the *Corriere della Sera,* Milan, of April 19, that Joan brings me last night, reminds me of William Morris, of Mark Twain. I do not say that the *radiofoto* looks like either the Englishman or the American, but I am reminded of them. *"Ezra Pound verso La Libertà."* The Ezra of the London period and the Ezra of my early American background are synthesized—as I am. There is also the Italy of his early affiliations, Rossetti and the Dante sequence. There is Dorothy Shakespear Pound "who technically brought the motion for dismissal of the indictment."

April 22, Tuesday

It was Friday, April 18 that the "indictment" was dropped. I find it very hard to catch up. I have not had time for meditation or day-dreaming and I need this. . . . It was on Friday, March 7 that I began these notes.

April 23, Wednesday

Now I hear from Norman with the press cuttings. He

wants me to send these notes for his secretary to type. "And now another canyon has been bridged by Ezra's end to torment. . . . I am glad you are writing it down, and Erich knows how important it is that you should write it down. . . . It is so good not to be hiding something—anything from those you love and who love you."

Thinking of Ezra's work, I recall my long *Helen* sequence. Perhaps, there was always a challenge in his creative power. Perhaps, even, as I said to Erich, there was unconscious—really unconscious—rivalry. My older brother was my mother's favorite; I, my father's. But the mother is the Muse, the Creator, and in my case especially, as my mother's name was Helen.

It all began with the Greek fragments—and living in seclusion in Lugano and Lausanne (and here, too) I finished, 1952, 1953, 1954, the very long epic sequence, my "cantos," as Norman called them.

April 24, Thursday

"I'm sorry I said you were hysterical. I was just worried." I was hysterical. "My only real criticism is that this is not my child." I could not scream in St. Faith's nursing home, March 30, 1919. I can not scream now. The train is rumbling nearer. The Child disappears. How did He come? How did He go? This was the summer before I went to America for my 70th birthday. I did not see Ezra and Dorothy. I did not want to see them. Now the "fiery moment," the whole creative output is centered on those two. He walked out of the gate, was she with him?

He is still there at St. Elizabeth's. He will stay five days more or so, I read in one of the papers that Norman sent. But, they said, he walked out alone. He took a walk alone. He walked into another dimension, as I do when I write of them. Dorothy is the *Bona Dea* of classic definition.

April 30, Wednesday

But there are others. Norman writes that Undine is going to Mexico. I look at Ezra's picture; this is an old man, they say. It is only by admitting that Ezra is an old man that I can say that I am an old woman. But this is not true. There are others. They go on painting pictures or they go on writing poetry.

What now? The curtain falls. I don't seem to see any further. They walk out, the battered Poet and the Faithful Wife. In my much-quoted "Weekend," Undine is reported to have said, "Grandpa loves me. It's because I symbolize the spirit of Love to him, I guess."

May 1, Thursday

"Grandpa loves me." That was long ago. There was Ishilda and the Tristram with the harp, the lyre. Long, long after, there was a new rôle, but it was the old Round Table. The music was incidental. As in the original legend, Lancelot, the bravest knight, was marred. But he remains the King's favorite. The Queen is a fortuitous character. But strength is given her. She meets the challenge, in the end. So separated, the characters synthesize, as I have said: Tristram-Odysseus, Lancelot-Achilles, each with the final partner, so balanced that they are almost one. And that having been achieved they retire from actual life; yet in their cloister, their country house or their remote *Castello,* they are working as toward a final unity.

May 7, Wednesday

Are they? I don't suppose it matters. Last Sunday's *London Chronicle* that George Plank sent me, reports an immediate blustering, "Roosevelt was a fool," a challenge to reporters who met him on a visit to the Congressman who had been most instrumental in his release, and a broad-cast on the BBC, reiterating the old, tiresome, outworn themes, sending his barbaric yap or yawp, like Walt Whitman, "over the roofs of the world."

This last picture varies in the process of reproduction. This is the photograph I first saw in the April 19 *New York Times* that Norman sent me, but showing the hand, clasping presumably, a spectacle case. "Testa Invocatrice"? Erich said of the *Corriere della Sera,* April 19, Milan, print that I had received earlier, that Ezra looked like Wotan. We are back with our Lupus or Lupa, the "Lady Loba." Our pard or panther, loosed finally from his cage, is still snarling. Would we have it otherwise? Erich bewails with me, however, the pity of it—"They might yet refuse him his passport"—but "this is psychologically inevitable," he says.

This last *London Chronicle* article balances the poet and his gifts with the wayward prophet. Where are we? We who have profited by his inspiration must take our stand—here, now.

May 8, Thursday

Actually, this is a premonition. Here is the legend. America has had Poe, localized; Whitman (for all his "cosmic" integration), localized; New England school, Emerson, Thoreau, localized; Emily Dickinson, localized. Here is the legend, the myth; actually, the basic myth can not be localized. Wotan, Odysseus or Herakles, born in Hailey, Idaho or wherever it is, educated in . . . wherever it was, and the young iconoclast finds himself in Venice, *le Byron de nos jours,* having been tacitly cold-shouldered by a distinguished section of a narrow slice of the American continent, in Philadelphia, because of a scandal, not very near, in Indiana, a very minor scandal, if a scandal at all.

It is the *feel* of things rather than what people do. It runs through all the poets, really, of the world. One of *us* had been trapped. Now, one of *us* is free. But we, the partisans of world-thought, of the myth, shiver apprehensively. What now?

I heard from Norman yesterday. He speaks of the original interview that was quoted in the *London Chronicle.* "It was really dreadful. As his friend Horton remarked (he is the Square Dollar man who took me to the hospital in Washington), 'one or two more interviews like that and the government will shanghai him out of the country.' "

May 9

I said when I first heard of Ezra's freedom, that he walked out of the gate of St. Elizabeth's alone, into another dimension. I was wrong. He walked out into the same dimension; that is, he seems to have walked out into life as he left it, 12 years ago. He goes on with "all the clichés," as Norman calls them, picking up the cudgels where he was forced to lay them down.

Who are these dummies, these ogres of a past age, these fearful effigies that wrecked our world, these devils, these dolls? Who are they? We put away childish things. It is we who walked into another dimension. Did they ever exist? Did Ezra ogre-ize himself by his association with Radio Rome? Joan laughed immoderately when I told her of Ezra's broadcast! Hitler and Mussolini flung at this late date into the very teeth of the British Lion!

It is funny. It isn't even sad.

No. It isn't sad. There is a reserve of dynamic or daemonic power from which we may all draw. He lay on the floor of the Iron Cage and wrote the *Pisan Cantos.*

Vidal,
Vidal. It is old Vidal speaking,

stumbling along in the wood,
Not a patch, not a lost shimmer of sunlight,
the pale hair of the goddess.

May 10

This is an earlier Canto (IV), it is true, but this theme
runs through the *Pisan* series and the later *Rock-Drill,* to
the end, so far, to 1955. This Canto IV is listed alone as
from the Ovid Press, London, 1919. That is the year that
Ezra came to St. Faith's Ealing, London, and stormed into
my room. A window looked out on a garden with rows of
crocuses and the first flowering trees. There *was* a Child,
there *is* a Child, implicit somewhere. Its image manifested
at the Stadelhofen station, Zürich, that summer day, before I went to America for my 70th birthday. Perhaps
Ezra "manifested" too, perhaps he never came to my room
and jeered at me. There was no tenderness. Perhaps there
was passion and regret "that this is not my Child."

I did not follow the course of the *Cantos,* listed in the
Eva Hesse *Dichtung und Prosa,* 1925, 1927, 1930, 1934. I
did see Ezra in Paris, once, twice (perhaps three times) in
those intermediate years. I did see him and for the last
time in London, after Mrs. Shakespear's death—was it
about the time of *The Fifth Decad of Cantos,* 1937?[39] Now,
Cantos LII–LXXI, 1940 and we are far apart.

The Children's Crusade by Marcel Schwob. . . .[40]

May 11, Sunday

I made that last entry yesterday. It flashed into my
mind, a book that I have not thought of, for perhaps 50
years. It was one of the little *de luxe* reprints of the Portland, Maine, Mosher series that Ezra brought me at the
time of the avalanche of Ibsen, Maeterlinck, Shaw, Yogi

books, Swedenborg, William Morris, Balzac's *Séraphita,*
Rossetti and the rest of them. It was the time of writing
"a sonnet a day when I brush my teeth," the time of the
lost *Is-hilda* book.

I am not sure of the spelling of Schwob and Joan looks
it up, but it is not in my reference book. "Children's Crusade," however, is there, 1212, and the 50,000 unarmed
children from France and Germany who set out to rescue
the Holy Sepulcher. Bryher, who is here, seemed shocked
that I did not know of Schwob, "He was associated with
the Mallarmé group—you must have heard Aldington and
Flint discuss him." I said, "I didn't always listen and I
can't remember everything." It is hardly a process of remembering, but almost, as I have said, of "manifesting."

May 12

"Writing down," Erich says, "is putting up all your de-
fenses against impopery—impropery or improperty—." I
suggest, "Impropriety." "Writing down is another defense. . . ."

The *Chronicle* spoke of Ezra collecting, appropriating,
stealing lines and phrases from Greek, Latin, mediaeval
and oriental poets, and building a nest like a magpie. It
asserted, however, that the effect was astonishing and
"make it new" had vitalized a host of lesser satellites. I
tell this to Erich but explain that I feel the process is that
of a Phoenix, rather than of a magpie. There is fragrance.
What did he write? "Myrrh and olibanum"? I said, "You
catch fire or you don't catch fire." There is the drift of in-
cense (almost perceptible in my room here) from the dim
gold cave-depth of St. Mark's and Santa Maria dei Miracoli, in Venice. That was the miracle, the Child that day
at the Stadelhofen station, "Christo Re, Dio Sole." Was
the Child that until then, I had not visualized, lurking,

hiding? It is the Child of Séraphitus-Séraphita. There are Mary de Rachewiltz and Ezra's grandchildren in Italy. There are my own daughter and my grandchildren in New York. Do I feel disloyal to them all? What am I hiding? "Good-bye, Dave, you'll come over Christmas Day, won't you?" Am I stealing, have I stolen? Is my own magpie nest a manger?

May 13

Norman writes, "Do keep on with the private E.P. notes. This is the moment on paper for a kind of catharsis, the ordering and getting it down which will free you. It is the ordering, not the data which is important." This letter is full of news, though Norman has not heard directly from the Pounds. I don't know why I feel restless, myself selfishly frustrated, when I read of their plans of sailing for Italy. Does it recall the first break when Ezra left, on a cattle-ship (I read somewhere) for Venice? Undine leaves or is to leave for Mexico, though not alone. I no longer identify myself with her, but I would like to help, via Norman, who is to keep her art treasures for her while she is away. I have no nostalgia for Aztec temples. If I am frustrated and jealous, it is because I myself am immobile, as far as travelling is concerned. They gossip too much, of course. Will Ezra rush off to Rome, Florence or Venice? But he can't, Norman writes, "for, after all, he is released in Dorothy's *custody*."

Custody? Marriage? "He might want to break away, for that very reason," said Erich. Did he want to break away from me? Of course he did. Was I hiding suppressed memories of that infinitely remote equivocal "engagement"? He broke it by subconscious or even conscious intention, the little "scandal," the loss of a job was intentional? Logically it was all impossible, we know that. So long ago . . . . , but the two-edged humiliation, from the friends and family, from Ezra, was carefully camouflaged, covered with the weeds and bracken of daily duties and necessities, and a bridge finally crossed the chasm or "canyon," as Norman called it, a forceful effort toward artistic achievement.

May 14

"And now another canyon has been bridged by Ezra's end to torment." *Ezra's end to torment*—that is all that matters. It is not easy to readjust, for it is only in retrospect that we dare face the enormity of the situation. There must be many others who feel as we do.

In Ezra's early poem, "The Goodly Fere,"[41] a tough Anglo-Saxon peasant fisherman tells the original Galilean story. He is the center of some kind of communal integration—disintegrating toward rebirth, as personally Ezra severed me (psychically) from friends and family. If having been severed, painfully reintegrated, we want only to forget the whirlwind or the forked lightning that destroyed our human, domestic serenity and security, that is natural. It is, in a sense, *sauve qui peut*.

I did not hear the raucous voice from Radio Rome. Friends listened and one especially, whose job it was to check up during the war on the BBC foreign broadcasts, said the effect was baffling, confused, confusing, and she didn't feel that the "message," whatever it was, was doing any harm or any good to anybody. It had, in a way, nothing whatever to do with us and the 20,000 victims of the first big air attacks and the fires in London. "Tudor indeed is gone and every rose."[42] No, Ezra!

May 15, Thursday, Ascension Day

To recall Ezra is to recall my father.

To recall my father is to recall the cold, blazing intelligence of my "last attachment" of the war years in London.

This is not easy.

Or it is easy enough in terms of *Helen and Achilles,* my 1952, 1953, 1954 "cantos," as Norman called them.

And all that time, and years before and years after, Ezra was in "torment," to use Norman's word. "And now another canyon has been bridged by Ezra's end to torment."

May 17, Saturday

He blustered his way in, he blustered his way out. Violet Hunt's very old mother, bedridden, with the door open at the head of the stairs, said fretfully, "Tell him to go away, tell him to go home, he always makes too much noise, that young Mr. Browning."

He wrote an opera, *Villon,* broadcast, I read [in "Weekend"], in 1932 by the BBC. At least, he hummed tunes or whistled them and they must have been transcribed by some musical expert. I did hear Olga Rudge, the accomplished violinist, play some Provençal fragments in London in the early days, (I did not pretend to follow them), presumably composed or resurrected by Ezra. He seemed unintimidated by the fact that (to my mind) he had no ear for music and, alas, I suffered excruciatingly from his clumsy dancing. I suffered, indeed I suppose we all did. He himself, in a certain sense, made no mistakes. He gave, he took. He gave extravagantly. Most of the tributes to his genius, his daemon or demon, have come, so far, from men. But at least three women, whether involved in the emotional content or not, stand apart; he wanted to make them, he did not want to break them; in a sense, he identified himself with them and their art.

May 18, Sunday

There is, in another category, Eva Hesse with the German translations and there is Sister M. Bernetta Quinn whose "The Metamorphoses of Ezra Pound" I found so illuminating. There is of course Mary, "the 32-year-old wife of Prince Boris de Rachewiltz," with her Italian translations of her father's *Cantos.*

Last night, I heard on AFN, that Ezra Pound, the American poet, is to sail for Italy on the *Cristoforo Colombo.*

May 20, Tuesday

The exact Séraphitus image has emerged, manifested from Texas. I am caught away by the *Time,* May 19, account of the young pianist, "Van [Cliburn] is a born flaming virtuoso."

"Lord, now lettest thou thy servant depart in peace." Music was what I wanted. "What are you hiding?" I was hiding a craving, a hunger for music, such as I had known it as a schoolgirl, at the old Academy in Philadelphia. Once, too shattered to move, after a concert by Paderewski, I found myself alone in the vast empty circle of balcony benches. Clinging to a rail, I was surprised to perceive below me a furtive handful of dark figures clustered in the empty half-lighted theatre before the vacated piano. These were not of the fastidious, fashionable audience that had just surged out. Who were these modest, dark-clothed figures, so far below me, hat in hand, in their overcoats, standing, though now the comfortable plush-covered parquet stalls were empty? Who are they, critics making obeisance to the vacated piano, the empty bench? Who am I? We are of a secret order. The theatre seems to grow darker. It is obvious that we should not be here. The Maestro returned.

The Maestro came back, it almost seemed that he sneaked back. We are "in" on this together. There in the dim light, he played for us for almost an hour. My head was on my arms. I did not cry easily. But I was crying. He was playing Liszt's symphonic setting of the *Erl King.*

Erl König, he was himself that Spirit. *O Vater, mein Vater.*

May 21, Wednesday

Prairie wild-fire—or what? It swept Russia, Leningrad, Moscow, "from Riga to Kiev," and ourselves are caught up in "the love-affair between Van and the Russians." What was an equivocal and terrifying enigma, the Soviet Union, becomes part of human consciousness, heart-consciousness. We need not torture ourselves with apprehension, a miracle has happened. I have laughed from time to time at Erich's reference to a German or Germanic philosophy, Klages' *Cosmogonic Eros.*[43] We have laughed together. But here it is, it seems. We had almost given up hope of world reconciliation, but America in the person of this strange overgrown maverick (as *Time* calls him) proclaims "These are my people, I guess, I've always had a Russian heart. I'd give them three quarts of blood and four pounds of flesh. . . ." This is familiar, evangelical. "Take, eat, this is my body." Van, it is said, approached the former Viennese conductor, Josef Krips, before a performance of the Buffalo Philharmonic Symphony, and said, "Maestro, let us pray." Van's prayer was, "God give us His grace and power to make good music together."

May 23, Friday

The Idol that should have been, that could have been, that was somehow "hidden," was, is the *Wunderkind.* If I was not the Child, as I obviously was not (as a child), I would have the Child. But the thought, the wish, the will was cosmogonic—and I use the word flippantly, one can't be too serious and it is a joke of Erich's and mine. Yes, yes—I never told him of it but the Child at the Stadelhofen station, that summer day, before I went to America for my

70th birthday, was the Child, the *Eros*. And the Van, this Vanya is the Child. There must be others, perhaps many others. And Ezra, at one time, was an Idol, an Image of its adolescence, in its Ariel or Séraphitus stage. And all this is long ago, and today, and tomorrow, and "existentialist" as Erich would say.

June 4, Wednesday

Yes, all this is today. I have been slowly and laboriously typing these notes, since May 24. In the meantime, Undine emerges. She is a reflection-in-a-mirror, Undine, ghost-like. This is a picture that Norman sent me with a number of photographs of her own drawings and paintings. She has asked him to keep these and some of "la ceramica," when she goes to Mexico. She took the photograph herself (of herself), reflected in the mirror, in a "bikini," Norman wrote. It is a graceful little body, and the triangular face belies Rattray's description in the "Weekend." No doubt, the young man was puzzled and disturbed at the apparition, "perched like a bird at dusk . . . with her golden hair falling down around her thin shoulders." As I reread the "Weekend," the description, in light of later events, becomes even more poignant and revealing. "I assumed that she was a patient from another ward." Norman writes that as he left St. Elizabeth's after his visit, Pound "told me he was not seeing her but gave no reason and still asked me to help her."

Norman wrote me, asking my advice about some of the pictures. I feel that we have inherited Undine.

June 5

"Pound threw his arms around her, hugged her, and kissed her goodbye." The second "Weekend" day, "Pound embraced her and ran his hands through her hair," and on leaving, "Pound embraced Undine as on the day before."

David Rattray writes, "She had huge eyes like a cat." He speaks of her enormous forehead, tiny chin and tinier double-chin. There is no suggestion of this chin discrepancy in the mirror. The face seems peaked, triangular, the soft hair pushed off and back from the high forehead. Both Erich and Joan were enchanted with the photograph and said that the impression of Undine conveyed by the "Weekend" seemed strangely distorted.

I see this Undine. Somewhere in *Rock-Drill,* Ezra writes of dry rocks, desolation, no water, no place for his Undine. When Ezra left finally for Europe, Frances came into my life. She completed or "complemented" the Dryad or Druid that Ezra had evoked so poignantly. Now, it almost seems that we have a super-imposition, as Ezra leaves or will leave or has left this Undine, again so poignantly evoked—but in what desolate surroundings.

June 6, Friday

Undine. "O swallow—my sister . . . the world's division divideth us . . ." off to strange adventure, looking for a Temple, an answer. I tremble at the words, Aztec, Aztlan, which Norman quotes from one of the letters . . . and a Tomb, a Venus, her own creation, to go with her— where? Frances Josepha completed me after her "father," as Undine calls Ezra, left America for Europe, in 1908. This is 1958. The year's division divideth us? No.

June 7, Saturday

Erich Heydt has filled in the "years' division." My own "weekend" is empty without him. He comes to see me at tea time (coffee time), as a rule, the first days of the week. Bryher comes on Tuesday and acquaintances from Zürich are due on Wednesday and Saturday. They want to spring-clean me out of my surroundings, one day next week. This is worse than a trip to Mexico. I can not "take" Aztec and Aztlan, though I wait feverishly for news from Norman.

June 8, Sunday

Feverishly? Is that the word?

Dorothy, the pillar of strength, the ivory tower, hides or tries to hide in her corner, "behind a ramshackle old upright piano." He and his Undine won't meet again. What did he say? It was a public occasion. They were all public occasions. The dim hall is always filled with the patients, the other patients, but they have their small, pathetic privacy, a semi-enclosed "alcove." There is a group of Negroes at a table, near by, and others lying on benches along the wall. Did he tell her, then and there, it was the last time, or did he leave it at that, and write one of his all but indecipherable letters, to be understood at least in that connection, "We won't meet again." They won't meet "outside." She has friends, work, she is not alone.

Why did she write Norman of herself, Undine, "He killed her"?

Yes, it was a public occasion. It must have been the last time I saw him, before he left for Europe. It was at the Burd School where we had had the dances and the coasting parties. "Father won't be back," Margaret [Snively][44] said, "you and Ezra can stay in his study." There was a couch. There were fiery kisses. There is a tentative knock. Ezra answers the door and turns to the heavy long velvet curtains. "What is the matter?" It was another shock, again "caught in the very act," such as it was. It was enough to draw an audience. The school girls, it was discovered, had assembled on the balcony above—one of them loyally had come across to their private apartment and told Margaret. There must have been a gap in the folds of heavy velvet; anyhow, the girls had had their peep-show. I was frozen, then. Now, I think of Undine, the last time at St. Elizabeth's, and the background of dark faces, a jungle.

June 11, Wednesday

Erich spoke of past, present and future, [Heidegger's] *die drei Ekstasen der Zeitlichkeit* when I read these last entries to him, yesterday. "Did you only just remember this last—peep-show?" "I couldn't really have forgotten it, but it only became real when I wrote of it; past, present and future, as you say, came together, *die drei Ekstasen.* This is the sort of remembering that is reality, *ecstasy.* The act of this remembering is an *ecstasy,* even if the thing remembered is as—"some dull opiate to the brain, and Lethe-wards had sunk."[45] But I couldn't sink to Lethe—the humiliation dragged me back." "That happened first with your father?" "Yes—yes—but somehow this second episode only comes *true* in relation to another ('he kissed her goodbye'), perhaps that is the future, this sort of remembering, *ecstasy."*

He said, "I am sad that you say your "weekend" is empty. I could always come on Saturday." I try to explain that the emptiness is part of it—part of last summer when he was gone for three months—part (only lately realized) of the emptiness when Ezra left America—and that realization came true, became *real,* only when I heard on April 18th, of Ezra's release and plans to return to Europe, and my ecstasy was tempered by my sympathy, identification almost, with Undine. I did not know then that they had already parted.

I show Erich a *Time* notice (June 9) that speaks of Ezra's

formal application for passport which was granted him. It speaks of "mad old poet Ezra Pound." Erich says, "But really, how wonderful—*mad old poet*—it's out of—out of—." *"King Lear,"* I say.

June 14, Saturday

I read an interesting article by Edmund Wilson, on "Mr. Eliot," in *The New Yorker* of May 24, 1958. Mr. Wilson writes of T. S. Eliot, "Of no other poet, perhaps, does Cocteau's bon mot seem so true, that the artist is a kind of prison from which the works of art escape." Mr. Wilson speaks of the compulsive drive of Eliot's poetry, he wrote under compulsion—as we write. The prison actually of the Self was dramatized or materialized for our generation by Ezra's incarceration.

June 19

There is an intermediate place or *plane,* however, that can not be ignored. It survives the memory of the first fiery Lupus and the "last attachment," a Panther of another order, the Ulysses and Achilles of heroic stature. It is *le paradis* of *laisser aller,* of the orange groves of Capri, of arcades and arches of Padua and Verona. Let go, it says, the grandiose, let go ambition; scribble and write, that is your inheritance, no grim compulsion.

Make no mistake. Poles apart, two poles made communication possible. Establish the poles. Others may use our invention, extension, communication. We don't care any more. Only, watching, a purely instinctive gesture impels us. We would reach out, snatch a victim from the altar. *Aztec. Aztlan.* What can we do about it?

June 20

As I have said, Norman sent me the photographs of her pictures. I had also Undine's booklet that Joan found me in Zürich. I wrote Norman of my feeling for her work, he wrote her of this. He said she would appreciate recognition from "another artist." So through Norman, I receive a letter from her and I write her direct. She writes me again. In this letter of June 9, I am all the things that I would forget, "seeress," "most high," "most beautiful" and all the rest.

She had a copy of *Modern American Poetry*,[46] she said, and in the H.D. section, she had made drawings in the margin. Should she send me the book?

June 21, Saturday

Undine seemed myself then, I wrote when I heard the April 18th broadcast—the *then*, however, extends in time. It is the creative pencil that reshaped a poem in the Museum tea room in London. The poem was "Hermes of the Ways." I wonder if this first published poem is in the book Undine wants to send me.

June 25

Poor Undine! They don't want you, they really don't. How shall we reconcile ourselves to this? . . .

Sentiment, sentimentality struggle with reason. . . .

June 26

Undine writes, "The male just can't go about like that, ditching a spirit love." She writes, "I have known Ezra for 6 years." She says, "The last 4 years I took a vow in St. Antony's Church in NYC not to leave the Maestro until he was freed. A month before he was freed he made me break that vow."

6 years? Where does that take us on the pattern-parallel, the map or graph? 1958—6 years—1952. That summer we began the long Helen sequence, an attempt, not unsuc-

cessful, to retain a relationship, materially "ditched." That is the only way to keep a vow. "But this is WAR," Undine writes. Mine was WAR too, transposed to the heroic, retaining sea-enchantment. Nothing is lost or can be, of what Undine calls "a spirit love."

June 27, Friday

On June 19, we wrote, "We would reach out, snatch a victim from the altar. *Aztec. Aztlan.*" A letter came yesterday from Norman. "Her [José Vasquez] Amaral[47] was taking her paintings to Mexico for an exhibition, there was a horrible accident in Texas, which killed his girl friend driving with him and wrecked the car. One gathers the art was destroyed, but she also speaks of now having to go there to get it."

I wrote Norman that I had had a premonition of disaster but did not want to write her of it. I wrote on June 7, "I can not 'take' Aztec and Aztlan, though I wait feverishly for news from Norman."

Is this the news? Has *Aztec, Aztlan* taken its victim? Will they let Undine go?

June 28, Saturday

Calendar days now have precedence and procedure. On June 10, Undine posted me the copy of *Modern American Poetry*. It has just come. It was sent from Washington, but the return address is given as Mt. Vernon Ave., Alex., Va. It must have been in her long June 9 letter that she spoke of the marginal sketches. But one is a full page drawing of Ezra, done over the "Evadne"[48] lines, "I first tasted under Apollo's lips / love and love sweetness, . . ."

I find the reference to [Vasquez] Amaral. "Now José Amaral, the Aztec, has given me another name . . . and I can not do other than use it."

There is a *Little Flower* pressed and carefully mounted on the initial page of the H.D. section.

We would like to confide Undine to the care of Marie-Thérèse-Françoise, Sainte Thérèse of Lisieux.

June 30

In the *Modern American Poetry,* Undine writes in the margin of the "sea-girls" section of T. S. Eliot's "The Love Song [of J. Alfred Prufrock]," " 'an old legend,' sayeth my mother, 'says that if a Sea Prince call us and we go live with him everything will be fine unless we can still hear human voices; if we do they immediately wake us from our enchantment and we drown.' I guess once you've decided to walk through a wall you shouldn't change your mind in the middle."

July 2, Tuesday

Undine is imposed or super-imposed on Frances [Gregg] Josepha, as I have said. Again, Frances was the Florence of my childhood—all boy's names. (Florence was a page or youth in the old French legends.) Florence—Frances. Frances said that people were always calling her Florence.

Florence was one of a family of sisters, like the little one of Alençon and Lisieux. I have difficulty sorting out the sisters. There was Marie, Pauline, Céline—and another, Léonie? Florence was a pretty child with the same crop of short curls that we see in the early Thérèse pictures. And our little Undine on her sea-rocks with her wind-blown hair, again, looks not unlike the early Florence. For myself, all three, the Saint, the rejected wild and willful Undine and the gracious *châtelaine* of Bon Air, Virginia (the childhood alter-ego from whom I was parted at 8) become one in consciousness, the "lost companion" who figures so prominently in many analytical case histories.

July 3

Lucie Delarue-Mardrus tells the Thérèse story from a reasoned worldly Protestant standpoint. This does not detract but adds to the overwhelming pathos of the legend. Thérèse was very young when she lost her mother, she turned to her older sister. When Pauline enters the Convent, Thérèse decides to follow her *petite mère.* She must wait 7 years until she is 16, before she can join Soeur Agnès or Mère Agnès de Jésus. Soeur Thérèse de L'Enfant Jésus lived there until she was 24.

I had heard of the *Histoire d'une Âme,* her short autobiography, just before War I, but I was not particularly interested. I heard in 1925 of the Vatican ceremony of the elevation of Thérèse, Soeur Thérèse. Sainte Thérèse had a peculiar talent. She would spend her heaven, she had promised, doing good on earth. She had thousands of clients. A friend (Protestant) during the second war, brought me a little string of 13 beads. "You say a Glory-be," she told me, "Glory-be-to-the-Father-and-to-the-Son-and-to-the-Holy-Ghost for each bead, eight days in succession—an octave—my Catholic sister-in-law told me. You can give half-a-crown to a beggar or put it in the poor-box, but it is not necessary. Just for extra, you can buy a rose and lay it on her altar (there is one at Brompton Oratory). You just tell your trouble or worry and ask for help. *It works.*" During the war the octaves—or was it novenas?—worked wonders.

For a long time after the war, I did not touch or "tell" the beads, but I came back to them.

Madame Mardrus says that she is the only one of the

thousands of admirers and clients of Sainte Thérèse who never asked for anything.

July 7

I have been reading Denton Welch. He died in 1948, at the age of 31, after a long illness due to criminally careless driving, another "horrible accident." He was a schoolboy, an art student, on a Whitsun holiday, on his bicycle, happy, free. Then everything went, he was lying in a field. *A Voice Through a Cloud*[49] tells this story, laconically, with touches of grim humor. There is authentic martyrdom; the record, with few if any allusions to "God-the-Father-God-the-Son-and-God-the-Holy-Ghost," almost has its place beside that of Thérèse's *Histoire d'une Âme*.

The boy himself has his place with the *Eros* we have named, that special Angel.

July 11

Now they have gone. The *bon-voyage* letter that I sent them through Norman, would not have reached them in time.

July 13

But I hear from Norman who saw them off on July 1, on the *Cristoforo Colombo*.

"Tuesday was an event! I went to New York to see Ezra and Dorothy off. He had written and asked me to go. I got to the Pier at 2:30 and after a little false search found my way to cabin 128, tucked away in a corner of first-class at the end of a corridor. The door was closed but Omar Pound opened it and greeted me, '*You* are the one we *want* to see. Come in!' The door closed behind me. There on the bunk lay Ezra, stripped to the waist, his torso rather proudly sunburned. At his knees on the bunk sat Marcella [Spann] shoeless. On the other side of the cabin was Dorothy, smiling and looking very well. She rose and kissed me, to my surprise; and I gave her a single yellow rose. 'H.D. wanted me to give you this,' I said. I told her you knew she was going but not when. 'You were commanded, then!' Dorothy said, and she was really touched. 'Yes,' I answered, for the Spirits had told me you did command.

"Eventually I discovered that Omar was a guard against the press who kept coming for photographs and interviews, neither of which was permitted. It was hot but cozy. Ezra was no different from ever. For half an hour he lectured me on college entrance examinations, and the program I must follow to improve them. He talked about Marcella Spann's and his anthology [*Confucius to Cummings*][50] and what I must do about it. He showed me Canto 99 which had just appeared. I will get you a copy eventually. And so it went. Then the whistle blew at 3:30 and we bade farewell. Ezra took both my hands and pressed them warmly; Dorothy gave three affectionate kisses to me and an invitation to Brunnenburg. 'Don't look so sad,' Ezra said.

"And so that is ended and I wonder if I shall ever see either of them again. And in any event your rose was with them. 'It is for the *Paradiso*,' I said at the end."

Notes to *End to Torment*

[1] Küsnacht. At the time of the composition (1958) of *End to Torment*, H.D. was staying in Küsnacht, Switzerland, where she was recovering from an injury due to a fall.

[2] Ignace Paderewski. The Polish pianist and composer (1860–1941).

[3] Erich Heydt. H.D.'s friend and doctor, the *Oberarzt* (chief doctor) of the Klinik Hirslanden near Küsnacht.

[4] *Formel*. (Literally, formula.) Pound had submitted H.D.'s first poems to *Poetry* (Chicago) under the signature "H.D. *Imagiste*," thereby providing

Hilda Doolittle with a pseudonym and the "imagist" movement in poetry with a formal title.

5 "Weekend with Ezra Pound" by David Rattray. This article, to which H.D. refers throughout *End to Torment,* was published as she notes in *The Nation,* November 16, 1957, pp. 343-49. In the article David Rattray, then a student of Provençal literature, reports on two days of visits with Ezra Pound at St. Elizabeth's Hospital in Washington, D.C. Others present during his conversations with Pound included Dorothy Pound, Jean Marie Châtel, and David Horton.

6 Ramon Guthrie poem. "Ezra Pound in Paris and Elsewhere," by Ramon Guthrie, is published together with the Rattray article in *The Nation,* November 16, 1957, p. 345.

7 Gaudier-Brzeska. Henri Gaudier-Brzeska was a young sculptor and friend of Ezra Pound in London. He was killed in World War I. Pound's study of his work, first published in 1916, was reissued in a revised and expanded edition by New Directions in 1960, under the title, *Gaudier-Brzeska: A Memoir.*

8 Klinik Hirslanden. The clinic near Küsnacht at which H.D. received care during her convalescence from a broken hip.

9 Frances Gregg [Josepha]. A childhood friend of Hilda from Philadelphia. They traveled to Europe together in 1911.

10 Richard Aldington. British poet, essayist, and translator. H.D. and Aldington were married in 1913, separated in 1919, and divorced in 1938. With Pound and H.D., Aldington was an original member of the "imagist" group of poets.

11 Bryher. Pen name (later legalized) of Winifred Ellerman, British novelist, and friend of H.D.

12 May Sinclair. British novelist, 1870–1946. *The Divine Fire,* London, 1904.

13 *Séraphita.* A mystical novella by Balzac, first published in 1835, whose protagonist is an androgynous figure variously called Séraphita or Séraphitus. Much of the book is devoted to an explication of Swedenborg's doctrines of theosophy.

14 *10ème Jour lunaire.* This prayer is quoted from *Le Kabbale pratique* by Robert Ambelain, Paris, 1951, p. 220.

15 *Merkur,* January 1958. The article by Peter Demetz, entitled *"Marginalien: Ezra Pounds Pisaner Gesänge,"* appeared in *Merkur,* January 1958, v. 12, pp. 97-100. It intersperses commentary on the *Pisan Cantos* with a report on a visit by Demetz with Pound, at St. Elizabeth's. He describes Pound's profile as that of a *Raubkatze* (predatory cat), and refers to him as *"den heimlichen Kaiser der amerikanischen Dichtung":* the hidden emperor of American poetry.

16 *15ème Jour lunaire.* From *Le Kabbale pratique* by Robert Ambelain, p. 222.

17 "They asked him to leave." Pound was an assistant professor of Romance languages at Wabash College, Crawfordsville, Indiana in 1907-1908. He did not fit in well at the small Indiana college (he later wrote that they considered him too much "the Latin quarter type": see Noel Stock, *The*

Life of Ezra Pound, New York, 1970, p. 43). He was asked to resign his position after a landlady discovered a woman in his rooms.

[18] "Maenad, bassarid." "Maelid and bassarid among lynxes," from the "lynx-hymn" of Canto 79.

[19] "strange spells of old deity." From "Cino," *A Lume Spento,* 1908. See the *Collected Early Poems of Ezra Pound,* New York, 1976, p. 10.

[20] Dorothy Shakespear. Pound met Dorothy Shakespear in 1909; they were married April 20, 1914.

[21] "There is a stir of dust from old leaves . . ." Canto 79.

[22] Mosher reprint. *The Romance of Tristram and Iseult,* retold by J. Bedier, tr. by H. Belloc, Portland, Me., Thomas Bird Mosher, 1907.

[23] *The Gadfly,* New York, 1897. A historical novel by Ethel Voynich (1864–1960), set in mid-19th-century Italy. It is strongly anticlerical; the hero, the illegitimate son of an Italian prelate, is involved in revolutionary activities, and also publishes political verse-lampoons for the Republican movement under the pseudonym "The Gadfly." His signature is the sketch of a gadfly with spread wings; he is slightly crippled, and as a youth spent some time as a "zany" in a traveling circus. He is eventually captured, court-martialed, and executed.

[24] *Ezra Pound, Dichtung und Prosa.* Trans. Eva Hesse, Zürich, Im Verlag der Arche, 1953.

[25] "pig stye." In 1954 Pound had written to H.D. concerning her interest in Freud: "You got into the wrong pig stye, ma chère. But not too late to climb out." Quoted in Pearson's foreword to *Tribute to Freud,* Boston, 1974.

[26] *Motive and Method in the Cantos of Ezra Pound,* ed. Lewis Leary, New York, 1954.   ,

[27] Frobenius. Leo Viktor Frobenius (1873–1938), German cultural anthropologist and archaeologist. Guy Davenport, "Pound and Frobenius," in Leary, pp. 33–59.

[28] *An Examination of Ezra Pound,* ed. Peter Russell, New York, 1950. In response to Peter Russell's request for an article in honor of Pound's 65th birthday, H.D. wrote a letter which contained a brief memoir of Pound, the seed of *End to Torment.* The letter was never published, and was eventually sold to H. Alan Clodd and then to Norman Holmes Pearson. It is now in the Collection of American Literature, Beinecke Library, Yale University.

[29] "San Cristoforo . . ." Canto 93.

[30] Undine. American painter who became a friend of Pound during the St. Elizabeth's years.

[31] *Poetry.* "An Exchange on Ezra Pound," *Poetry,* XCI, 3 (December 1957), pp. 209–11. The correspondence concerns the poor quality of the F.B.I. transcripts of Pound's broadcasts on Rome Radio and the consequent merits of the treason charge placed against him.

[32] "Helen and Achilles." *Helen in Egypt,* New York, 1961.

[33] "Pomona, Pomona. Christo Re, Dio Sole." Cantos 79 and 82.

[34] "Arche Verlag." *Dichtung und Prosa,* ed. Eva Hesse, Zürich, 1953.

[35] *A Lume Spento, 1908–1958,* Milan, 1958. A selection from Pound's

earliest published poems, with a few poems from the San Trovaso Note-book of 1908.

36 "Venetian Night Litany." In *A Quinzaine for this Yule* (1908); see the *Collected Early Poems of Ezra Pound,* p. 60: "Night Litany." The autograph manuscript, to which H.D. refers, was published in facsimile in *A Lume Spento, 1908–1958.*

37 "she danced like a pink moth in the shrubbery." From "Au Jardin," *Canzoni* (1911); see *Collected Early Poems,* p. 174.

38 Undine's little book. Published in Milan; a small booklet of reproductions of paintings, with an introduction by Ezra Pound.

39 Mrs. Shakespear's death. Olivia Shakespear, Dorothy Pound's mother, died in October 1938. *The Fifth Decad of Cantos,* London and New York, 1937.

40 *The Children's Crusade* by Marcel Schwob, trans. H. C. Greene, Portland, Me., 1905. A book of prose-poems written from the viewpoint of various participants in the Children's Crusade of 1212. (First published, Boston, 1898.)

41 "The Goodly Fere." "Ballad of the Goodly Fere," *Exultations,* 1909; see *Collected Early Poems,* p. 112.

42 "Tudor indeed is gone and every rose." Canto 80.

43 "Klages' *Cosmogonic Eros.*" Ludwig Klages, *Vom Kosmogonischen Eros,* Jena, 1930.

44 Margaret Snively [Pratt]. A friend of H.D. and Pound in Wyncote.

45 "some dull opiate to the brain, and Lethe-wards had sunk." See Keats's "Ode to a Nightingale": "Or emptied some dull opiate to the drains / One minute past, and Lethe-wards had sunk."

46 *Modern American Poetry,* ed. Conrad Aiken, New York, 1927. See illustration, p. 59.

47 José Vasquez Amaral. Friend of Pound and Undine; translator of the *Cantos* into Spanish.

48 "Evadne." In *Selected Poems of H.D.,* New York, 1957, p. 38.

49 Denton Welch, *A Voice Through a Cloud,* London, 1951.

50 *Confucius to Cummings.* Ed. Ezra Pound and Marcella Spann, New York, 1964.

"HILDA'S BOOK"

"Hilda's Book" is a small (13.7 cm. × 10.5 cm.) book, hand-bound and sewn in vellum, of 57 leaves (first leaf handwritten on vellum), with vellum closures. Due to heat or water damage, the first (vellum) leaf has fused to the paper leaf behind it (partially obscuring the poem beginning, "I strove a little book," which has been deciphered with the help of another manuscript in the Pound Archive of the C.A.L., Beinecke Library, Yale University). The last paper leaf has also fused to the back vellum. The title, "Hilda's Book," is handwritten in black ink, in ornamental script, on the front cover. It has partially faded with time.

All but two of the poems are typed, with a blue ribbon; the first poem ("Child of the grass") is handwritten in black ink in ornamental script on the opening vellum leaf, and some of the final words have worn away with age. Another poem ("Sancta Patrona") is handwritten on the verso of leaf 55 (following the second page of "The Wind"), perhaps as an afterthought.

Pound's corrections to the poems are handwritten in black ink or red pencil, often obscure because of smudging or fading. Where possible I have followed Pound's notations in establishing the texts of the poems, although some readings are uncertain because of multiple corrections or illegibility of the notes due to age. A few of the poems show extensive handwritten revision, but most are typed fair copies.

The poems in "Hilda's Book" were composed during

the first years of Pound's friendship with Hilda Doolittle, 1905–07, the period recalled in her memoir, *End to Torment*. Four of the poems were later published, with some changes, in Pound's early volumes: "La Donzella Beata," "Li Bel Chasteus," "Era Venuta" (as "Comraderie"), and "The Tree." The poem entitled "To draw back into the soul of things. Pax" is included in another version ("Sonnet of the August Calm") in the San Trovaso Notebook of 1908, as is "The Banners" ("Fratello Mio Zephyrus"). The poems from the San Trovaso Notebook are published in the *Collected Early Poems of Ezra Pound* (New York, 1976). Variant readings and publication histories of the early poems are given in the notes to that book. The poems of "Hilda's Book," and others in the San Trovaso Notebook, are among many other early poems addressed to Hilda (as "Is-hilda" or "Ysolt") which remain unpublished, and are now in the Pound Archive at Yale.

M.K.

Child of the grass
The years pass Above us
Shadows of air All these shall Love us
Winds for our fellows
The browns and the yellows
　　　　Of autumn our colors
Now at our life's morn. Be we well sworn
Ne'er to grow older
Our spirits be bolder At meeting
Than e'er before All the old lore
Of the forests & woodways

Shall aid us: Keep we the bond & seal
Ne'er shall we feel
     Aught of sorrow

        [. . .]

     Let light [?] flow about thee
     As [. . . ?] a cloak of air [?]

I strove a little book to make for her,
Quaint bound, as 'twere in parchment very old,
That all my dearest words of her should hold,
Wherein I speak of mystic wings that whirr
Above me when within my soul do stir
Strange holy longings
That may not be told
Wherein all autumn's crimson and fine gold
And wold smells subtle as far-wandered myrrh
Should be as burden to my heart's own song.
I pray thee love these wildered words of mine:
Tho I be weak, is beauty alway strong,
So be they cup-kiss to the mingled wine
That life shall pour for us life's ways among.
Ecco il libro: for the book is thine.

Being alone where the way was full of dust, I said
      "Era mea
      In qua terra
      Dulce myrrtii floribus
      Rosa amoris
      Via erroris
      Ad te coram veniam"

And afterwards being come to a woodland place where the sun was warm amid the autumn, my lips, striving to speak for my heart, formed those words which here follow.

La Donzella Beata

Soul
Caught in the rose hued mesh
Of o'er fair earthly flesh
Stooped you again to bear
This thing for me
And be rare light
For me, gold white
In the shadowy path I tread?
Surely a bolder maid art thou
Than one in tearful fearful longing
That would wait Lily-cinctured
Star-diademed at the gate
Of high heaven crying that I should come
To thee.

The Wings

A wondrous holiness hath touched me
And I have felt the whirring of its wings
Above me, Lifting me above all terrene things
As her fingers fluttered into mine
Its wings whirring above me as it passed
I know no thing therelike, lest it be
A lapping wind among the pines

Half shadowed of a hidden moon
A wind that presseth close
        and kisseth not
But whirreth, soft as light
Of twilit streams in hidden ways
This is base thereto and unhallowed . . .
Her fingers layed on mine in fluttering benediction
And above the whirring of all-holy wings.

Ver Novum

Thou that art sweeter than all orchards' breath
And clearer than the sun gleam after rain
Thou that savest my soul's self from death
As scorpion's is, of self-inflicted pain
Thou that dost ever make demand for the best I have to
    give
Gentle to utmost courteousy bidding only my pure-purged
    spirits live:
Thou that spellest ever gold from out my dross
Mage powerful and subtly sweet
Gathering fragments that there be no loss
Behold the brighter gains lie at thy feet.

If any flower mortescent lay in sun-withering dust
If any old forgotten sweetness of a former drink
Naught but stilt fragrance of autumnal flowers
Mnemonic of spring's bloom and parody of powers
That make the spring the mistress of our earth—
If such a perfume of a dulled rebirth
Lingered, obliviate with o'er mistrust,
Marcescent, fading on the dolorous brink

That border is to that marasmic sea
Where all desire's harmony

Tendeth and endeth in sea monotone
Blendeth wave and wind and rocks most drear
Into dull sub-harmonies of light; out grown
From man's compass of intelligence,
Where love and fear meet
Having ceased to be:

All this, and such disconsolate finery
As doth remain in this gaunt castle of my heart
Thou gatherest of thy clemency
Sifting the fair and foul apart,
Thou weavest for thy self a sun-gold bower
By subtily incanted raed
Every unfavorable and ill-happed hour
Turneth blind and potently is stayed
Before the threshold of thy dwelling place

Holy, as beneath all-holy wings
Some sacred covenant had passed thereby
Wondrous as wind murmurings
That night thy fingers laid on mine their benediction
When thru the interfoliate strings
Joy sang among God's earthly trees
Yea in this house of thine that I have found at last
Meseemeth a high heaven's antepast
And thou thyself art unto me
Both as the glory head and sun
Casting thine own anthelion
Thru this dull mist
My soul was wont to be.

To One That Journeyeth with Me

"Naethless, whither thou goest I will go"
Let, Dear, this sweet thing be, if be it may
But hear this truth for truth,
Let hence and alway whither soe'er I wander there I know
Thy presence, if the waning wind move slow
Thru woodlands where the sun's last vassals stray
Or if the dawn with shimmering array
Doth spy the land where eastward peaks bend low.
Yea all day long as one not wholly seen
Nor ever wholly lost unto my sight
Thou mak'st me company for love's sweet sake
Wherefor this praising from my heart I make
To one that brav'st the way with me for night
Or day, and drinks with me the soft wind and the keen.

Domina

My Lady is tall and fair to see
She swayeth as a poplar tree
            When the wind bloweth merrily
Her eyes are grey as the grey of the sea
Not clouded much to trouble me
            When the wind bloweth merrily
My Lady's glance is fair and straight
My Lady's smile is changed of late
            Tho the wind bloweth merrily
Some new soul in her eyes I see
Not as year-syne she greeteth me
            When the wind bloweth merrily

Some strange new thing she can not tell
Some mystic danaan spell
        When the wind bloweth merrily
Maketh her long hands tremble some
Her lips part, tho no words come
        When the wind bloweth merrily
Her hair is brown as the leaves that fall
She hath no villeiny at all
        When the wind bloweth merrily
When the wind bloweth my Lady's hair
I bow with a murmured prayer
        For the wind that bloweth merrily
With my lady far, the days be long
For her homing I'd clasp the song
        That the wind bloweth merrily

Wind song: this is my Lady's praise
What be lipped words of all men's lays
        When the wind bloweth merrily
To my Lady needs I send the best
Only the wind's song serves that behest.
        For the wind bloweth merrily.

The Lees

There is a mellow twilight 'neath the trees
Soft and hallowed as is a thought of thee,
Low soundeth a murmurous minstrelsy
A mingled evensong beneath the breeze
Each creeping, leaping chorister hath ease
To sing, to whirr his heart out, joyously;
Wherefor take thou my laboured litany
Halting, slow pulsed it is, being the lees

Of song wine that the master bards of old
Have left for me to drink thy glory in.
Yet so these crimson cloudy lees shall hold
Some faint fragrance of that former wine
O Love, my White-flower-o-the-Jasamin
Grant that the kiss upon the cup be thine.

Per Saecula

Where have I met thee? Oh Love tell me where
In the aisles of the past were thy lips known
To me, as where your breath as roses blown
Across my cheek? Where through your tangled hair
Have I seen the eyes of my desire bear
Hearts crimson unto my heart's heart? As mown
Grain of the gold brown harvest from seed sown
Bountifully amid spring's emeralds fair
So is our reaping now: But speak that spring
Whisper in the murmurous twilight where
I met thee mid the roses of the past
Where you gave your first kiss in the last,
Whisper the name thine eyes were wont to bear
The mystic name whereof my heart shall sing.

Shadow

Darkness hath descended upon the earth
And there are no stars
The sun from zenith to nadir is fallen
And the thick air stifleth me.
Sodden go the hours
Yea the minutes are molten lead, stinging and heavy

I saw her yesterday.
And lo, there is no time
Each second being eternity.
Peace! trouble me no more.
Yes, I know your eyes clear pools
Holding the summer sky within their depth
But trouble me not
I saw HER yesterday.
Peace! your hair is spun gold fine wrought and wondrous
But trouble me not
I saw her yester e'en.
Darkness hath filled the earth at her going
And the wind is listless and heavy
When will the day come: when will the sun
Be royal in bounty
From nadir to zenith up-leaping?
For lo! his steeds are weary, not having beheld her
Since sun set.
Oh that the sun steeds were wise
Arising to seek her!
The sun sleepeth in Orcus.
From zenith to nadir is fallen his glory
Is fallen, is fallen his wonder
I saw her yesterday
Since when there is no sun.

ONE WHOSE SOUL WAS
SO FULL OF ROSE
LEAVES STEEPED IN
GOLDEN WINE THAT THERE
WAS NO ROOM THEREIN
FOR ANY VILLEINY—

The Banners

My wandring brother wind wild bloweth now
October whirleth leaves in dusty air
September's yellow gold that mingled fair
With green and rose tint on each maple bough
Sulks into deeper browns and doth endow
The wood-way with a tapis broidered rare—And where
King oak tree his brave panoply did wear
Of quaint device and colored
The dawn doth show him but a shorn stave now.
If where the wood stood in its pageantry
A castle holyday'd to greet its queen
Now but the barren banner poles be seen
Yea that the ruined walls stand ruefully
I make no grief, nor do I feel this teen
Sith thou mak'st autumn as spring's noon to me.

"To draw back into the soul of things." PAX

Meseemeth that 'tis sweet this wise to lie
Somewhile quite parted from the stream of things
Watching alone the clouds' high wanderings
As free as they are in some wind-free sky
While naught but thoughts of thee as clouds glide by
Or come as faint blown wind across the strings
Of this odd lute of mine imaginings
And make it whisper me quaint things and high
Such peace as this would make death's self most sweet
Could I but know, Thou maiden of the sun,
That thus thy presence would go forth with me
Unto that shadow land where ages' feet

Have wandered, and where life's dreaming done
Love may dream on unto eternity.

Green Harping

Thou that wearest the doeskins' hue
"Hallew!" "Hallew!"
Tho the elfin horn shall call to you
'true   be true
By the violets in thy leaf brown hair
'ware   be ware
Tho the elfin knights shall find thee fair
'ware   too fair
Tho hosts of night shall hail thee queen
   In the Eringreen
The elf old queen hath sorrow seen
and teen   much teen
Tho the shadow lords shall marshall their might
   afore thy sight
Hold thou thy heart for my heart's right
   in their despite
Tho night shall dwell in thy child eyes
'wise   be wise
That thy child heart to mine emprise
'plies   replies
For night shall flee from the fore-sun's flame
'shame   in shame
Tho my heart to thee embeggared came
'same   'tis the same
That lordship o'er the light doth hold
'bold   quite bold
And thee to my kingdom I enfold
By spell of old.

From another sonnet.

THY FINGERS MOVE AGAIN ACROSS
    MY FACE
AS LITTLE WINDS THAT DREAM
BUT DARE IN NO WISE TELL THEIR
    DREAM ALOUD—

Li Bel Chasteus

That castle stands the highest in the Land
Far seen and mighty
—Of the great hewn stones
What shall I say?
And deep foss-way
That far beneath us bore of old
A swelling turbid sea
Hill-born and torrent-wise
Unto the fields below, where
Staunch villein and wandered
Burgher held the land and tilled
Long labouring for gold of wheat grain
And to see the beards come forth
For barley's even-tide.

But circle arched above the hum of life
We dwelt, amid the
Ancient boulders
Gods had hewn
And druids runed
Unto the birth most wondrous
That had grown

A mighty fortress while the world had slept
And we awaited in the shadows there
While mighty hands had laboured sightlessly
And shaped this wonder 'bove the ways of men.

Meseems we could not see the great green waves
Nor rocky shore by Tintagoel
From this our hold
But came faint murmuring as undersong
E'en as the burgher's hum arose
And died as faint wind melody
Beneath our gates.

The Arches

That wind-swept castle hight with thee alone
Above the dust and rumble of the earth:
It seemeth to mine heart another birth
To date the mystic time, whence I have grown
Unto new mastery of dreams and thrown
Old shadows from me as of lesser worth.
For 'neath the arches where the winds make mirth
We two may drink a lordship all our own.
Yea alway had I longed to hold real dreams
Not laboured things we make beneath the sun
But such as come unsummoned in our sleep,
And this above thine other gifts, meseems
Thou'st given me. So when the day is done
Thou meet me 'bove the world in this our keep.

Era Venuta

Some times I feel thy cheek against my face
Close pressing, soft as is the South's first breath

That all the soft small earth things summoneth
To spring in woodland and in meadow space
Yea sometimes in a dusty man-filled place
Meseemeth somewise thy hair wandereth
Across my eyes as mist that halloweth
My sight and shutteth out the world's disgrace
That is apostasy of them that fail
Denying that God doth God's self disclose
In every beauty that they will not see.
Naethless when this sweetness comes to me
I know thy thought doth pass as elfin "Hail"
That beareth thee, as doth the wind a rose.

The Tree

I stood still and was a tree amid the wood
Knowing the truth of things unseen before
Of Daphne and the laurel bow
And that god-feasting couple old
That grew elm-oak amid the wold
'Twas not until the gods had been
Kindly entreated and been brought within
Unto the hearth of their hearts' home
That they might do this wonder thing.
Naethless I have been a tree amid the wood
And many new things understood
That were rank folly to my head before.

Being before the vision of Li Bel Chasteus

"E'en as lang syne from shadowy castle towers
"Thy striving eyes did wander to discern
"Which compass point my homeward way should be."

For you meseem some strange strong soul of wine . . .

Hair some hesitating wind shall blow Backward as some
    brown haze
That drifteth from thy face as fog that shifteth from fore
    some
Hidden light and slow discloseth that the light is fair—

Thu Ides Til

O thou of Maydes all most wonder sweet
That art my comfort eke and my solace
Whan thee I find in any wolde or place
I doon thee reverence as is most meet.
To cry thy prayse I nill nat be discreet
Thou hast swich debonairite and grace
Swich gentyl smile thy alderfayrest face
To run thy prayse I ne hold not my feet.
My Lady, tho I ne me hold thee fro
Nor streyve with thee by any game to play
But offer only thee myn own herte reede
I prey by love that thou wilt kindness do
And that thou keep my song by night and day
As shadow blood from myn own herte y-blede.

L'Envoi

Full oft in musty, quaint lined book of old
Have I found rhyming for some maiden quaint
In fashioned chançonnette and teen's compleynt
The sweet-scent loves of chivalry be told
With fair conceit and flower manifold

Right subtle tongued in complex verse restraint
Against their lyric might my skill's but faint.
My flower's outworn, the later rhyme runs cold
Naethless, I loving cease me not to sing
Love song was blossom to the searching breeze
E'er Paris' rhyming had availed to bring
Helen and Greece for towered Troy's disease
Wherefor, these petals to the winds I fling
'Vail they or fail they as the winds shall please.

The Wind

"I would go forth into the night" she saith.
The night is very cold beneath the moon
'Twere meet, my Love that thou went forth at noon
For now the sky is cold as very death.
And then she drew a little sobbing breath
"Without a little lonely wind doth crune
And calleth me with wandered elfin rune
That all true wind-born children summoneth
Dear, hold me closer! so, till it is past
Nay I am gone the while. Await!"
And I await her here for I have understood.
Yet held I not this very wind—bound fast
Within the castle of my soul I would
For very faintness at her parting, die.

Sancta Patrona
          Domina Caelae

Out of thy purity
Saint Hilda pray for me.

Lay on my forehead
The hands of thy blessing.
Saint Hilda pray for me
Lay on my forehead
Cool hands of thy blessing
Out of thy purity
Lay on my forehead
White hands of thy blessing.
Virgo caelicola
Ora pro nobis.

Rendez-vous

She hath some tree-born spirit of the wood
About her, and the wind is in her hair
Meseems he whisp'reth and awaiteth there
As if somewise he also understood.
The moss-grown kindly trees, meseems, she could
As kindred claim, for tho to some they wear
A harsh dumb semblance, unto us that care
They guard a marvelous sweet brotherhood
And thus she dreams unto the soul of things
Forgetting me, and that she hath it not
Of dull man-wrought philosophies I wot,
She dreameth thus, so when the woodland sings
I challenge her to meet my dream at Astalot
And give him greeting for the song he brings.